What peo
about *The Great Revitalization*

The bottom line is this: people crave meaning and purpose through work. It's high time business leaders got serious about fostering workplaces where people feel valued, cared for, and part of the shared purpose. Alise's latest provides both the inspiration and the action plan to revitalize both your leadership and your business.

> Bob Chapman, CEO of Barry-Wehmiller and author of
> *Everybody Matters: The Extraordinary Power of Caring for Your People Like Family*

While there have been many books on purpose, of which Alise's first book, *Purpose Ignited,* is a great read, this book goes multiple steps further. Her GUSTO NOW framework is an actionable plan putting the reader on a path towards revitalizing their company. The key points at the end of each chapter help to reinforce the concepts and evolve this into a how-to instead of being only a feel-good read. Lastly the topic of spiritual intelligence or SQ left me with much to ponder about my own organization's spiritual intelligence.

> Paul Drew, Co-founder and SVP of StackPath

The Great Revitalization is a thoroughly researched, deeply insightful and highly actionable guide to what has become a business imperative: igniting purpose in our businesses. As a purpose advisor to companies, I know that many leaders struggle to find answers on this topic. Does purpose really matter at my company? How do I reconcile organizational purpose with employee personal purpose? Which tactics are fluff, and which are evidence-based? Without oversimplifying, *The Great Revitalization* answers these (and most!) purpose-related questions. It synthesizes the world's relevant collective wisdom into an illuminating blueprint on running a meaningful business. Best of all, the book's guidance doesn't limit itself to today's best practices. Instead, it draws on the world's most inspired thinkers to point us toward a future in which capitalism has evolved into its sustainable, just, and higher state.

Bea Boccalandro, corporate purpose advisor and author of *Do Good at Work: How Simple Acts of Social Purpose Drive Success and Wellbeing*

A deep, shared sense of purpose is vital for individuals and organizations to channel their energies towards identifying and achieving long-term goals. If you are looking for a starting point to discover your mission, guided by a sense of purpose, look no further! This book is another feather in Alise's cap as she helps the reader navigate through the "what" and "how" of purpose driven leadership.

Atul Thatte, artificial intelligence and technology leader

Dr. Alise Cortez is an engaged, thoughtful leader. Her inspirational writings and podcasts will help you exceed your goals. More importantly, your purpose and passion will be forever enhanced... grateful!

Cary A Israel J.D., executive advisory board and consultant for CampusWorks Inc. and District President Emeritus at Collin College

We spend a lot of time at work, where you impact your team, your company and the whole business ecosystem. Alise shows us delicate and challenging concept application to our business goals and daily life. The Great Revitalization is a rare jewel and a staple book on business, personal and ESG topics.

Hoshi (Hoshiko) Kamiya Brooks, licensed and registered interior designer seeking ESG applications to the built environment

With *The Great Revitalization*, Alise conquered a complicated challenge – she summarizes and curates the best concepts out there in what I call the conscious transformation ecosystem. If you are starting on the journey or you have been on it for a while, this book is a great guide to identify the most important players, principles, and frameworks that will accompany you and your organization.

Francisco Fernández, Executive Director of the Conscious Enterprise Center at Tec de Monterrey

For a leader on the meaning and purpose journey, *The Great Revitalization* delivers a comprehensive and approachable process to enliven and modernize your business's eco-system through servant leadership and developing a purpose so clear and engaging stakeholders cannot help but follow. Alise distills her research, including conversations with key thought leaders, into a compelling approach to leadership, leaving breadcrumbs for further investigation with these important voices. This book serves as a beautiful dose of Alise's mentoring in book form.

Samantha Anderegg-Boticki, an ever-evolving leader with a passion for strong corporate citizenship and Global Director, Business Development at Modine Manufacturing Company

Alise is always bringing forth excellent tidbits of wisdom to help inspire and motivate leaders. She's delivering that value yet again in *The Great Revitalization*. This book will give you the push needed to passionately pursue the purposeful life hidden in your heart!

Justin McCorkle, a fellow student of life, business, and purpose

Filled with hard-earned wisdom, Alise has written a GUSTO-filled book that is sure to revitalize your business. In an age where so many businesses are trying to find their own unique way through a complex world and a cluttered marketplace, Alise shows readers how to travel a vital path and create a business that's purposeful, lasting, and yes, even beautiful.

Steven Morris, brand and culture building expert, CEO of Matter Consulting, and author of *The Beautiful Business: An Actionable Manifesto to Create an Unignorable Business with Love at the Core*

In times of upheaval, thoughtful leaders blaze paths to revival and sustainability. With *The Great Revitalization,* Dr. Alise Cortez has reimagined the events of The Great Resignation as opportunity knocking. With compelling insight and a deep understanding of the new economic rules, she lays down practical advice for leaders navigating organizations, and the people who comprise them, through daunting times toward unity and ultimate success. Regardless of which sector or industry you work in, you'll lead with clearer vision, build stronger teams and achieve higher levels of success after you've read *The Great Revitalization* and put Cortez' real-world advice to work.

T.D. Smyers, Captain, US Navy (ret), Founder, Principal and Executive Coach at A Bold Leader and CEO of Simple Leadership Strategies

Dr. Alise Cortez is offering all leaders a reminder packaged in the form of a gift. The reminder is of the interconnected structure of reality and of the human condition. We humans belong to each other. The gift is how pointedly she makes this point. As you read this book, it will become starkly clear that we are the cavalry we've been waiting for and the time to act is now.

Dr. Robyn Short, Founder/CEO of Workplace Peace Institute and author of *Peace in the Workplace: Transforming Conflict into Collaboration*

The great resignation taught us that the workforce is searching for meaning and purpose in everything they do. *The Great Revitalization* is a brilliant guide to creating business and organizational cultures around purpose and meaning. This book is a valuable reminder of what organizations can be and what we want them to be. Alise Cortez brings her GUSTO to our hearts and then adds meaning to it. *The Great Revitalization* is a framework to help us and others achieve our authentic purpose. I recommend this book to everyone, regardless of your status in any organization.

Danny Barton, Chief of Police at Coppell Police Department

THE GREAT REVITALIZATION

REVITALIZATION

HOW ACTIVATING MEANING AND PURPOSE
CAN RADICALLY ENLIVEN YOUR BUSINESS

ALISE CORTEZ, PHD

First published in Great Britain by Practical Inspiration Publishing, 2023

ISBN   9781788603850   (print)
       9781788603874   (epub)
       9781788603867   (mobi)

Every effort has been made to trace copyright holders and to obtain their permission for the use of copyright material. The publisher apologizes for any errors or omissions and would be grateful if notified of any corrections that should be incorporated in future reprints or editions of this book.

Want to bulk-buy copies of this book for your team and colleagues? We can introduce case studies, customize the content and co-brand *The Great Revitalization* to suit your business's needs.

Please email info@practicalinspiration.com for more details.

Practical Inspiration
Publishing

Other books by Alise Cortez, PhD

Purpose Ignited: How Inspiring Leaders Unleash Passion and Elevate Cause

Passionately Striving in "Why": An Anthology of Women Who Persevere Mightily to Live Their Purpose

Coloring Life: How Loss Invites Us to Live More Vibrant Lives

Dr. Doug,

To living with passion
and working in purpose!
Dr. Alie

Dedicated to all who align with Rabbi Harold Kushner's
observance that:

Most people are not afraid of dying; they are afraid of
not having lived…. It is not the prospect of death that
frightens most people. People can accept the inescapable
fact of mortality. What frightens them more is the dread of
insignificance, the notion that we will be born and live and
one day die and none of it will matter.

Table of Contents

Acknowledgments .... *xvii*

Foreword by Dr. Lance Secretan .... *xix*

Introduction: First Aid for the Exhausted,
Overwhelmed, or Lost Leader xxi

PART 1: THE "WHAT" OF GUSTO 1

Chapter 1 – G: Gumption – Your Business as an
Enlivening Force for Good (What) 5
    Your Business Can Breathe Vital Life Back into You 6
    Conscious Capitalism, the Superhero to Power
    Your Business 8
    Your Beautiful Business, Intelligently Designed 11
    The Long Play in Business 13
    Key Points Summary 16

Chapter 2 – U: Urgency – Wake Up and Turn Fast!
(When and Where) 19
    From Autopilot to a Constant Drive for Improvement ... 21
    The Cry for Work-Life Harmony 23
    The Call for Well-Being amid a Mental Health Crisis.... 27
    Fluid Location and the New Focus on Where
    Work Gets Done 29
    Key Points Summary 31

Chapter 3 – S: Sustainability in an Interdependent
World (Why) 33
    On Becoming Wise Homo Sapiens 35

Your "Living Organization" in Today's Stakeholder
Capitalism World 37
From an "Ego Economy" to a "Living Economy" 38
Sustainability and ESG as a Business Imperative 41
Key Points Summary 45

Chapter 4 – T: Therapy that Enlivens Hearts and Souls
Through Meaning (How) 47
The Workforce Hungers for Deep Meaning 48
Enter Logotherapy: The Surprisingly Simple Path to
Activate Meaning 49
The Playground of Work – Where Meaning is
Delightfully Activated 54
Doctor's Orders: Motivate Through Meaning 56
Key Points Summary 59

Chapter 5 – O: Ownership Culture that Unites All
Stakeholders Through Purpose (Who) 61
What is Purpose, and Why Does it Matter? 62
Purpose as Today's Driving Business Imperative 66
Your Parliament of Purpose 68
Key Points Summary 75

PART 2: THE "HOW" THROUGH NOW 77

Chapter 6 – N: Nurture Through Mindfulness (IQ) 83
Perform a Human Capital Process and
Procedure Audit 85
Focus on and Nurture Individual Strengths 87
Banish Your "High Performance" Programs and
Embrace "Momentum" 89
Re-Tool Feedback and Recognition 91
Measure and Increase Employee Engagement
and Fulfillment 93
Deconstruct Time and Place in Today's Nimble
Workplace 94
Elevate Your Team by Leveraging AI and Robotics 98
Key Points Summary 100

Chapter 7 – O: Open the Heart (EQ) 105
   Become a Caring Leader Who Celebrates "Everyone
   Matters" 107
   Managing Through Meaning™....................................108
   Bring Passion Back to the Workplace.........................112
   Inspire "Love in Work" and Spread Joy......................113
   Stomp Out Fear and Toxicity.......................................116
   Encourage Social or Job Purposing............................119
   Increase Relational Connection and Belonging
   Through DEIB 122
   Live the ESG+R Standard Every Day...........................124
   Key Points Summary..126

Chapter 8 – W: Wake the Soul (SQ) 131
   Do the Work – Be a Leader Worth Following.............133
   Add Inspiration to Evolve Your Leadership Practice..137
   Detect Your Company's Purpose – Your Unique
   Way of Being and Serving 140
   Embed Your Company Purpose into Every
   Operational Aspect..145
   Help Your Team Members Discover Their
   Own Purpose..148
   Elevate Your Company Purpose with Beauty 150
   Accept the Summons of Syntropy – Reaching to
   Our Higher Potential 154
   Key Points Summary..158

Conclusion 163

Select Bibliography..167

Endnotes...181

Index...195

Acknowledgments

Bringing a book to life does not happen without a lot of guidance, support, and inspiration. A hearty thank you to Linda Crompton, Mark Snyder, Atul Thatte, Charles Irsch, Hoshiko Brooks, Justin McCorkle, Carey Israel, and Nimesh Shah for their feedback on the early manuscript. It is no small feat to slog through the initial thinking of a book, and I am grateful for their generous contribution of time and effort to develop the ideas rendered. This work would not have sprung to life without the inspiration I receive from the *Working on Purpose* radio guests who grace the program each week. I thank the Public Relations professionals who send prospective guests and the authors and subject matter experts whose works I devour in preparation for the show. It is largely from studying the works of my radio guests that this book is in your hands. Finally, I thank my daughter Gabi for being a constant source of love and stability in my life.

Foreword
by Dr. Lance Secretan

It's the rare person who can fully comprehend just how much the playing field of business has changed in the early 2020s. The forces of the global COVID pandemic, unprecedented upheavals in social and political unrest, and a workforce rapidly evolving to be comprised of the millennial and Z generations are a few of the pressing issues wreaking havoc on business today. It's no surprise leaders feel overwhelmed and at a loss to navigate forward. Their tried-and-true methods no longer serve, yet it's dizzying to make sense of the new landscape terrain that has emerged. The workforce increasingly seeks employers offering flexibility through remote or hybrid options, and meaningful work at a company serving from its purpose. Indeed, it's a tough time to be a leader. In my five decades of teaching leadership in organizations across the world and having written 24 books on the importance of creating inspiring organizational cultures, I'm clear on two things: leaders must constantly keep learning to stay fit for their task, and the most effective approach to leadership is to inspire people. Indeed, inspiration is even more important than leadership.

This book is not for everyone. Its ambitious agenda to elevate conscious leadership and business is for those leaders who are either at their wits' end trying to run their companies in today's increasingly demanding times, or the forward-thinking ones who seek to become more inspired and therefore more inspiring for others. There are so many archaic practices that hamper the human spirit still governing how companies are run, something I addressed in *The Bellwether Effect* and many of my other books. Alise has done a masterful job of laying out the playing field of today's business confronting leaders. Reading it will help you understand the sheer forces you must address to run your company today and steward you to success. So as not to leave you hanging, she then offers best practices to not only bring you up to date but catapult you into an elevated consciousness journey to raise your awareness about the impact your company can have. Buckle up. This is not your typical business or leadership book. It's fresh and flirtatious, edgy and elevating.

Alise believes work should be a place to realize one's potential, yet it's just the opposite for so many people. She is out to help companies create cultures where people want to come to work and do their best who are led by inspirational leaders at companies doing business that makes the world better. She has built her expertise over 25 years of human capital consulting to companies, and her forte is helping companies activate meaning and purpose in their culture. Alise is a constant student of life and work (they are not separate!) who folds her ongoing studies into her consulting and writing. She has a unique vantage point through hosting the Working on Purpose radio program as it affords her a perch into the latest thought leadership on business and leadership. She is voracious in her preparation for her weekly radio shows, which keeps her sharp as a thought leader and consultant. Hers is a voice that teaches, inspires, and empowers.

Dive into a world of fresh thinking that will reignite your passion for leading with heart!

Dr. Lance Secretan, mentor and coach to leaders
and bestselling author of *Reawakening the Human Spirit*
and 23 other books

Introduction:
First Aid for the Exhausted, Overwhelmed, or Lost Leader

On an early Monday morning in March 2022, I sat across from Mychele Lord, Founder of Lord Green Strategies, in Dallas for our standing leadership meeting. I had been working with her team since Fall of 2021 to fold their purpose into their culture, develop inspirational leaders, and grow the team in numbers and competencies to bring them into an even more vibrant state of operations. While waiting for the rest of the team to join us, Mychele asked me casually, "So, what did you do this weekend?" Not thinking about it much, I replied, "Oh, I spent the weekend working on my next book." Surprised and curious, she followed up with, "What's it about?"

"It's a book to help leaders who are at their wits' end trying to navigate this new business world we find ourselves in during the Great Resignation and can't keep their people, don't quite understand how to engage their hearts and minds, and are just at a loss."

"You mean, you are writing a book about what you are doing for us here at my company," she said matter-of-factly. A delightful wave of appreciation washed over me that not only do I get to live my purpose doing the management consulting work I do today, but that Mychele immediately registered the value of our work together and recognized it as such.

Yes, I wrote this book for you, the weary traveler. Or, perhaps, curious, reaching learner. I'm glad to be on your journey with you as you navigate unprecedented times. Whether you're an owner of a business or leader of an organization or department of a small to mid-sized company, whether you've been in your role for three months or three decades, I'm guessing you've picked up this book because you are looking for some enlightening guidance and some encouraging support to keep you moving in a productive direction in these incredibly challenging and overwhelming times. When have you seen such high turnover, low engagement, and high stress in your organization? With so much swirling around you and new issues to confront, it can be hard to know which way to direct yourself, let alone your organization. Everyone needs a hand up. No one becomes their best without guidance, inspiration, examples, and the instruction of others.

I wrote this book to help you make sense of a changed world, as I've learned greatly from my radio show guests, and introduce you to what I hope will be some novel ideas stitched together in an accessible way to strengthen your organization's performance, and inspire and encourage you to reach for completely new heights in your business and as a leader.

Here's what you need to know. Work is powered by purpose and fueled by meaning. Find ways to activate those two and you are on your way to the Great Revitalization. This book is going to show you why this is an imperative and how to realize this promising future.

At the time of writing, the last few years have brought incredible havoc on the world. It's hard to imagine any aspect of life that hasn't been touched in some way by the COVID-19 pandemic. Economic recession rang across the world in 2020 and 2021 as the pandemic marched on. The global fighting and atrocities in Ukraine, Yemen, North Korea, and other countries tear into our united social fabric as loved ones are lost, property is destroyed, and economies impossibly ravaged. Social unrest in the United States escalated at the murder of George Floyd, as increasing numbers of all ethnicities across the globe supported the Black Lives Matter movement.[1] The global unrest is palpable, and the United States is increasingly a nation politically divided.[2]

People across the globe have reconsidered how they wish to live, who they are connected to, and on what terms they want to work. As people became sick with the virus or lost loved ones to it, a clarity about a closer version to an idealized life emerged for many people.[3] More people are opting for continued remote work or a hybrid environment of workplace and home. In this more fluid work environment, others have chosen to flee high-cost cities in favor of quieter and less expensive geographies where they can still enjoy challenging professional careers but in the locale of their choice.

Many company leaders have struggled with how to manage, motivate, and stay productively connected to a virtual workforce. Those working from home, in the early days of sheltering-in-place and ongoing throughout the course of the pandemic, found themselves needing to find a viable place at home from which to work and be productive. They faced a cacophony of competing interests – pets who voiced their needs and appreciation for their owners being at home with them and children who once were away receiving their education in a school now also "home schooled" while attending virtual classes, and competing for WiFi bandwidth.

As the pandemic wore on, staggering numbers of mental health and well-being declines have been registered across the population. People craved meaningful social connection, especially during the periods of sheltering-in-place. The world's population was forced to reevaluate every aspect of life, which ushered in a heightened thoughtfulness. A kind of post-traumatic growth seems to have occurred as people struggled through and emerged from the hugely challenging situation COVID presented. Survivors of such hardship gained a new wisdom and now see life and its opportunities with a renewed appreciation. The encouraging news for the world is that the pandemic has stirred people to want more from their lives, a sentiment Dr. Ranjay Gulati shared with me in our on-air conversation on my *Working on Purpose* radio program.[4] The challenging part for business leaders is translating into their operations that people are increasingly wanting "more" and "different" work. This seemingly new wanderlust is proving to be quite vexing for the companies and leaders who depend on attracting, engaging, and retaining those souls to power their organization.

These people, disconnected from vital relationships and focused on many competing fronts, are the same ones you, the leader, have been trying to keep motivated and supported during the last few years. Meanwhile, those same exhausted people have been in increasing numbers feeling disconnected from their companies, but still wanting to develop their careers. This perfect storm has contributed to what has been termed the "great resignation," a phenomenon where people are leaving their jobs, often without another one yet secured.[5] Maurer predicted that half the workplace in North America would change jobs in 2021, a phenomenon that has played out in real life for many companies, adding insult to injury to companies still reeling from the pandemic struggles.

As jobs go unfilled for longer periods, employers are learning they must increase pay to attract workers, as employees are increasingly unwilling to work for minimum or low wages. Companies recognize their employees' disconnect from them in their lack of engagement, performance, innovation, and retention – in general, lackluster business results. The Gallup organization defines employee engagement as the involvement and enthusiasm of employees in both their work and workplace and reports that the average engagement among worldwide employees is appalling at 20%.[6] Matt Johnson of Motive X says employee engagement is the lagging indicator of performance in companies, not a leading one. Engagement is the "middle man," and motivation is the root cause of engagement (or lack thereof). Motivation is best accessed and activated through meaning and purpose, and you'll learn ways to do so in Part 2 of this book.

Why this book, now? The newly emerging world comes with dizzying change, leaving business leaders completely baffled as to how to proceed. I sit across from leaders who are at a complete loss in dealing with the droves of people exiting their organization, while those remaining are dealing with mental health and stress issues not seen before, along with a workforce wanting much more freedom and autonomy. As the volume of these desperate voices continued to rise, I kept having one fascinating conversation after another on my weekly *Working on Purpose* radio program about how the world of work was changing. The barrage of information came through several other channels. The message was deafening, but how to make sense of it and respond? This book is my humble offering to help you make sense of all that noise and usher in a much brighter future for your business than you ever imagined.

The message and tools offered in this book are informed from my education and consulting experience. I've spent 25 years working in the human capital industry, the last five of which have been served as a management consultant stewarding meaning and purpose inside companies. My education includes a PhD in Human Development (where I studied meaning in work for my dissertation and found 15 Modes of Engagement) and Logotherapy, which centers on healing (and revitalizing) through meaning. I've been hosting the weekly *Working on Purpose* radio program since February 2015, which has proven to be an ongoing "university study" for me. The program is a thought leadership platform that advances the conversation on creating workplaces where people actually *want* to come to work and do their best; where inspirational and caring leaders lead people to discover their greatest potential, and robustly profitable business is done to better the world. Looking at the contents of the program from its inception, you can recognize they are a reflection of the unfoldment of my own consciousness and purpose expression. I'm dedicated to realizing my highest potential to serve my listeners/viewers and clients and delight in the accompanying fulfillment.

I then continually fold in these ideas to my practice of management consulting and have continued doing so as I've learned over the years. I've had the privilege of helping steward the journeys of my clients using what I've learned to enable and empower their journey toward purpose and a lively, engaged workforce. These pages are your invitation to join the Great Revitalization being stewarded in this book. The Great Resignation and these extremely challenging business times have forced a "boot" upstairs for leaders. Most of us don't mind being elevated – that is, learning, growing, and transforming – it's just that it's usually a terribly messy process. The question is "how"? The answer is finding your GUSTO as a leader and company, and activating it NOW, which is what this book is all about.

What's GUSTO, you ask? Most people I've asked over the years readily respond with such words as: enthusiasm, zest, fervor, energy, delight, glee, or zeal. I like them all. You'll learn why as you read along, but the actual word "gusto" is one that registers quite meaningfully to me. Because I lived in Spain and Brazil in my 20s and speak Spanish and Portuguese, respectively, "gusto" has the distinction of meaning something readily identifiable along the lines mentioned above in those languages as well as English. Finding your gusto, then, is not only motivating to me, but, as I've continued to come to understand, is becoming increasingly a necessary tool for anyone who needs energy to deal with vexing challenges as well as to pursue magnificent opportunities.

To familiarize you with some key terms used throughout the book, here are some definitions to situate you to the book's content.

Meaning: That which registers to you as important or significant, and usually in alignment or an expression of your values, which energizes you in your experience or encounter with it.[7]

Purpose: Always aimed at serving or helping others.[8]

    a) *Individual:* Your rare and unique reason for existing that betters the world.[9]

    b) *Company:* The reason the organization exists and why anyone should care.

Logotherapy: An existential psychology practice that recognizes humanity's chief concern and primary motivation is meaning and uses principles to awaken and enable individuals to connect to their sources of meaning to vitalize their well-being.

Conscious capitalism: The integration of belief in pro-capitalism and systems improvement, personal and business advancement, and social and environmental impact.

Stakeholder capitalism: A growing worldwide reform movement that creates returns for investors by creating value for employees, customers, supply chain and distribution partners, communities, and the environment. It replaces shareholder primacy as a principle of corporate governance.

This book is comprised of two parts: Part 1 is focused on helping you find your GUSTO in your business or company; Part 2 teaches you how to activate it NOW. Thus, Part 1 helps you fully understand the ecosystem that has been evolving over the last few tumultuous pandemic years and *what* the opportunity is that awaits you as a leader or business owner. Part 2 provides tools and best practices for *how* to respond productively to take you and your company to a whole new level – and realize your own version of "the Great Revitalization."

PART 1: *What?*
    G – gumption (what)
    U – urgency (when and where)
    S – sustainability (why)
    T – therapy (how)
    O – ownership (who)

PART 2: *How?*
    N – nurture (IQ)
    O – open (EQ)
    W – wake (SQ)

Chapter 1 opens with "What" – the idea that the answer to today's business demise is an enlightened business which has activated its spirited initiative by completely and fully operating from its purpose, representing the "G" of GUSTO. Another way to describe "gumption" is a "shrewd or spirited initiative or resourcefulness" or "the ability to decide what is the best thing to do in a situation, and then do it with energy and determination" (Cambridge Dictionary online). Boldly, I concur with many other business leaders and scholars that business is the best hope to solve humanity's pressing problems and doubly wins when it achieves a way back to health and revitalization. The questions of "when" and "where" are answered in Chapter 2, as the "U" of "urgency" is unveiled through a reveal of the pressing forces shaping today's world and workforce that require swift action. People have learned they want "more" from work and life than they did pre-pandemic, and the companies that employ them are scrambling to meet that demand.

    The "S" of GUSTO in Chapter 3 concerns the "why" of "sustainability" in an interdependent world of stakeholders, which ultimately allows for a path toward resiliency and vitality. Here, sustainability speaks to a viable business that is enabled to continue successful operations *and* does so in ways that are mindful of environmental, social, governance, and resilience

(ESG+R) company initiatives to help protect and preserve the planet's health. Realization of the Great Revitalization is not possible without stewarding sustainability, as the Earth will continue to exist – the question is how and whether its inhabitants will fare as humans go about living and running companies. "How" to revitalize the human agents who power business toward this optimal level of health is achieved through "T," or "therapy", logotherapy to be specific, as discussed in Chapter 4. Logotherapy offers healing (and vitalizing) through the activation of meaning, and the opportunity for companies to create a culture that enables all team members to activate it themselves. Doing so infuses vital energy in each person while encouraging them to take direct ownership of their engagement, performance, and ultimately the development of their career, a set of tasks which are often otherwise unduly expected of managers and leaders.

The last chapter of Part 1 discusses the "O" of GUSTO, the "who," the full complement of "owners" in any business, otherwise known as stakeholders, who are united and fortified through the platform of company purpose. Not at all the common "slathering" of purpose, but *real* and *deep* purpose that is the operational *soul* governing all decisions and activities of the business. Intentionally and meaningfully uniting all stakeholders – employees, suppliers, investors, the community, and the planet – produces a behemoth shared commitment to the company's purpose, ultimately producing a unified whole of synchronous beating hearts that is greater than the sum of its parts. The result? A force of upward reach that unleashes all manner of motivation, innovation, perseverance, and performance.

Having fully articulated the components of *what* comprises GUSTO for companies, Part 2 addresses *how* to activate it NOW through best practices that awaken and activate meaning, purpose, and connection among stakeholders. Its three substantive chapters are organized along the continuum of evolved intelligence types in the business world:

IQ, EQ, and SQ – or intelligence quotient (with a focus on logic and rationality), emotional intelligence, and spiritual intelligence. Starting with performing an audit of all your human capital processes and procedures, Chapter 6 provides a robust set of practices to mindfully "nurture" the people who power your organization. From banishing your "high potential" programs, to retooling feedback and recognition, better utilizing artificial intelligence and other technologies to remove monotonous tasks, and playing the strategic long game in business, this chapter guides you in key aspects of evaluating and reshaping your everyday operations to elevate the experience of your team members.

You'll learn specific ways to open and engage the hearts of your stakeholders through the "O" of NOW in Chapter 7. Starting with caring leadership that whets the appetite to reach for their own stars, this chapter contains numerous practices to awaken passion in your workforce, remove harmful fear, and increase vital relational connection among your stakeholders. From helping team members learn to access meaning in the simple moments of life, to identifying ways to inject "social purpose" into their daily work, and on to facilitating their recognition of unique talents and strengths, there is a wide array of methods informed through logotherapy and purpose to revitalize your company. You achieve this by enrolling the hearts of your people so they feel like owners with "skin in the game" in keeping your company strong and successful.

Bringing it all back to the vantage point and actions of you the owner or leader, Chapter 8 addresses the "W" in NOW by "Waking" all your stakeholders to their higher consciousness and aligning and expanding their individual purpose through that of your organization. It is extremely motivating and fulfilling for people to feel part of something greater than themselves and thus feel enlarged by their affiliation. Creating a culture where your stakeholders are invigorated by your company purpose and clearly understand how their daily tasks support its realization opens a spigot of near unstoppable force. As you make it safe and accessible for anyone connected to your business to experience, without fear or embarrassment, more of the full gamut of human emotions – like hopefulness, joy, and awe – you elevate the human experience of working through vitalized and enlivened hearts and minds. Along the way, you are inviting the development of resilience and perseverance toward the realization of goals. When work becomes a place where people can be fully "human" and even experience love at work, individual lives as well as the bottom line become revitalized. The four-part transformational process prescribed in this chapter will help you get there: awaken, agitate, activate, and apply, a process that can be used repeatedly as you take your company to ever-increasing heights.

Each chapter of the book contains references to authors cited, further reading suggestions, and examples to illustrate key points from *Working on Purpose* radio show guests. Various episodes are referenced for you to find online, as my program is livestreamed to my *Working on Purpose* Radio TV YouTube channel and then syndicated to 28 other audio platforms like iHeart Radio, iTunes, Stitcher, etc. A Key Points Summary completes each chapter, and at the end of each chapter in Part 2 you'll find a checklist to help you put into practice the NOW best practices.

Does this sound like a lot of work? You bet. Is it worth the journey to figure it out and run fast and hard on this path? You bet your life. And that of your company. The final chapter is your invitation to keep reaching *high* by fully operating your business from its magnificent purpose to see what could lie beyond today's way of operating a business. Your "beautiful business" beckons and invites you to step into its full potential.[10] You will learn that as you steward your own consciousness journey as a leader and as a business, the beauty and contribution you can make is positively mesmerizing. Business – your business – can be *such* a force for good in the world, especially when stewarded by a conscious, inspirational, and caring leader like you. Enjoy the journey.

PART 1
The "What" of GUSTO

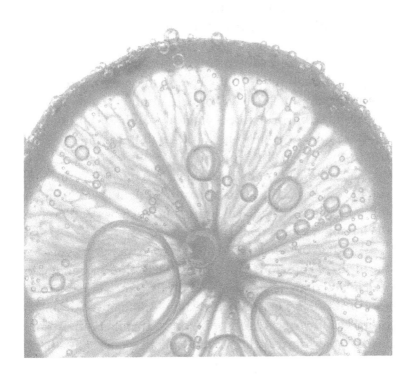

The chapters in Part 1 introduce the components required to play in the new world of business in the 2020s. This book begins where my previous book *Purpose Ignited: How Inspiring Leaders Unleash Passion and Elevate Cause* left off – its ending promise chapter. You will become acquainted with the opportunity to elevate consciousness by drawing on principles of conscious capitalism, stakeholder capitalism, logotherapy, meaning, and purpose.

Imagine the promise of business as the Conscious Capitalism organization encourages its practitioners:

> Their higher state of consciousness makes visible to them the interdependencies that exist across all stakeholders, allowing them to discover and harvest synergies from situations that otherwise seem replete with trade-offs. They have conscious leaders who are driven by service to the company's purpose, all the people the business touches, and the planet we all share together. Conscious businesses have trusting, authentic, innovative and caring cultures that make working there a source of both personal growth and professional fulfillment. They endeavor to create financial, intellectual, social, cultural, emotional, spiritual, physical and ecological wealth for all their stakeholders. (www.consciouscapitalism.org/)

The vision of Conscious Capitalism is one I hope inspires you to your core, as a purpose realized ought to do. Imagine this possibility, and you will spring into each day determined to champion such a reality.

Another organization that has given powerful voice to the ideals of conscious capitalism is the Business Roundtable, which describes itself as a non-profit association of chief executive officers of America's leading companies working to promote a thriving US economy and expanded opportunity for all Americans through sound public policy. On August

29, 2019 the organization announced the release of a new Statement of Purpose of a Corporation that moves away from shareholder primacy and embraces a commitment to *all* stakeholders.[1] Signed by 181 CEOs who commit to lead their companies for the benefit of all stakeholders – customers, employees, suppliers, communities, and shareholders – it raised quite a debate among dissenters. Arguments have been raised against it, declaring the impossibility of serving more than one master, that being the shareholder. Others smirk that once an economic downturn occurs, these "enlightened" business leaders will turn right back to old practices of cutting staff and costs to maintain bottom-line business results to stay in good stead with shareholders. Yet, even in the midst of the COVID-19 pandemic, as companies struggled with reduced revenues, there were many instances of CEOs either taking a substantial pay cut or foregoing salaries altogether in order to retain more employees.

It's critical you remember that you have something magnificent to draw energy and inspiration from and to build on – your business. You have abundant resources in the products or services you provide and the people you employ to bring them to market. You are positioned to do so much good in the world, and I hope reading this book enables you to be even more successful in today's changed business landscape.

To aid you on this journey, in Part 1 of the book, I'll explain what GUSTO is and take you through the constituent parts of the acronym: Gumption, Urgency, Sustainability, Therapy, and Ownership. These five topics correspond respectively to the exploration of What, When and Where, Why, How, and Who, which will help you to discover vital meaning and purpose in your business.

You will benefit greatly by detecting your company's purpose, or revisit it as it's likely evolved over time. Your community stakeholders are selective about who they do business with. You can make your business more beautiful and more impactful with an intentional, conscientious design.

The answer is enlightened business through conscious, caring leadership practiced through conscious capitalism, which has found its gumption – the topic we will explore in Chapter 1 – by completely and fully operating from purpose.

The business world – including consumers – is the ideal sphere to manage this major revolution in leadership. Business can best handle it. The reach and power of its experience, infrastructure, and resources, combined with social and exponential technologies, mean that we in the business world have never been better equipped to find, enable, and execute world-changing solutions.[2] Your access to this revitalization is anchored in gumption, discussed next in Chapter 1.

1

G: Gumption – Your Business as an Enlivening Force for Good (What)

Where *has* your "get up and go, gone up and went?" It's been a grueling few years since the COVID pandemic first hit, and so much of the way the world operates and business is done has changed. Quite likely, forever. It is easy to lose your connection to "what" you and your business stand for as the multiple pressures of running it commingle. It has been bewildering for many leaders to press onward in what has arguably been one of the most challenging times experienced, with the global pandemic shutdown, supply chain issues, and evolutions in the workforce demands. There have got to be days, maybe weeks and months, that you ask yourself just why it is *you* stay in the leadership role you're in given the enormity of challenge you face to run your business.

Enter the promise and power of "gumption," a spirited initiative, enlivened through purpose. The opportunity is focus, where you put it, and how you allow yourself to be governed by its aim. It is essential you are clear about "what" it is you're up to through your business. To kickstart your company's way toward the Great Revitalization, first, put your own oxygen mask on. Only then will you be able to help lift others in your organization and across your stakeholder communities. To do so requires you to reconnect, or connect more deeply, to your own conviction that you are committed to steering your business or company forward. Set your intention, grab your courage, summon your "guts," and set on down the trail.

Relax. You got this. To start down the path to finding your gumption, this chapter opens with some fresh perspective on how you can relate to your business and frame your stance on what it's doing to be of service to customers. It encourages you to look for ways to "fall in love" with your company all over again, just as you can in your personal relationships. You'll learn that adopting this view can vitalize your capacity to tackle the business changes you face more adeptly and creatively. You will learn how embracing conscious capitalism can fortify your convictions and elevate your thinking and business planning for greater outcomes. By operating from the long-term view of realizing your company's purpose and considering the needs and wishes of all stakeholders while enrolling them into your company's purpose, you will find your own spirits bolstered while positioning your company to create greater value for everyone.

Your Business Can Breathe Vital Life Back into You

When you first fully recognize that your business, department, or company is not just an "entity" with (perhaps) buildings, products or services, and customers, but a living organization that requires nurturing and can grow or decay,[1] you begin to understand how you and the business can breathe life into each other. Your business or company is a pulsating organism that needs attention, care, and nourishment to grow and become more profitable, and efficient ways to collect and dispense with its waste. Your business or company has a *heartbeat*. And a soul, something we'll delve into more deeply in Chapter 8.

Norman Wolfe muses that when you look beyond the necessary aspects of profit and loss statements and all the other operational aspects that go along with running a business, and open your vista to something bigger, inspiration awaits. "If we could change the way business related to its role in society, to its customers, and to its employees, we could make a very large and very real difference." When asked what the vision of his book and leadership development practice is today, Wolfe says, "It is to transform business around the world into environments that support and enhance the dignity of the human spirit as they collectively express this spirit in service to society."[2] With *that* kind of wind in your sails, do you think you could summon a little more conviction and determination to steward your business forward?

Deborah Westphal takes this notion a step further. She says people are demanding you stop the divergence between how and why your business exists. You can find answers by considering how time, change, chance, connectivity, constellations, and conflict affect the currents of humanity, technology, today's archaic organizations, and tomorrow's human-centric businesses. But first you must ask the questions. Give yourself time to step back and look at beliefs, behaviors, and actions currently residing in your organization and within yourself.[3] A framework for getting started exists, and it begins with the realization that immense energy exists within the human system. In other words, it's imperative that you look for the beauty and what's already good and right in your business and set a determination to prize and celebrate it. It can be hard to remember the qualities of your business when you've been struggling to continue operating and remain profitable, especially as the Great Resignation and other business pressures continue to plague you.

Finding your gumption as a business requires both time for reflection and unleashing a certain conviction to work toward the path that lies ahead. If you're like many leaders, you've experienced fear, doubt, uncertainty, and bewilderment, to name just a few beleaguering emotions. In her book and our on-air conversation, Alicia Hare discovered for her own leadership journey and that of her company a new navigational system for how she could live and lead. Taken together, these building blocks create what she calls "The Unfolding Path" which involves managing fear, embracing choice, working from purpose, and focusing on brighter futures. What she has found is available to you – to become more able to create a powerful cycle that builds on itself. Hare says: "The more I live and lead from this different way, the more I find my inner stability and power, the more I step into the fullness of who I am and who my life wants me to be, the more I fully shine."[4] You can apply this same approach and activate awareness with and through the business you own or the company you lead.

Conscious Capitalism, the Superhero to Power Your Business

Recognizing that your company or business department likely has a larger capacity for innovation, contribution, and growth can be quite invigorating. This is true on any scale, whether your entity has a handful of employees and customers or several thousand. You can use this realization to whet your appetite for possibilities awaiting your company and begin to power through the next set of perplexing challenges. When you consider just what you can do with your business, you are positioned to take action by looking for ways to design your business to do all manner of good.

A shining spokesperson for conscious business is Dr. Raj Sisodia, who I've featured on the *Working on Purpose* program.[5] The author of 13 books on business and strategy, Dr. Sisodia is also the co-founder of the global Conscious Capitalism movement.[6] With an anchor organization in San Francisco and various membership organizations in cities across the world, the movement recognizes that capitalism is a fundamentally human endeavor and conscious capitalism is the integration of pro-capitalism and systems improvement, personal and business advancement, and social and environmental impact. Its four tenets are designed to elevate humanity through business by operating with higher purpose, stakeholder orientation, conscious leadership, and conscious culture. I've personally experienced Dr. Sisodia's programs and message and have humbly served as an adjunct teacher (facilitating in Spanish) in a program he and Dr. Neha Sangwan ran to teach conscious capitalism principles to Latin American CEOs. In a book he coauthored, the authors put forward that once someone understands that capitalism can evolve to meet genuine human needs, creating value, being of service to one another, *and* fulfilling people's own self-interests in a much richer, deeper way, why would you consider doing anything else and settling for less?[7] Adopting this stance will not only lift your own spirits but also attract and retain like-minded stakeholders who believe in your mission and how you're working to achieve it. There was a time in the not-so-distant past when stakeholders were largely synonymous with investors and customers.[8] Today, companies are best served when they consider the full community of stakeholders, including employees, suppliers, the community or society, and the planet, in addition to the two previously focused upon. According to Westphal, business was more benevolent until the 1980s when it began to move away from civic belief and move more toward serving the shareholders. The redefinition of the purpose of a corporation offered by the Business Roundtable moves corporate governance away from shareholder primacy to include a commitment to all stakeholders, to invest in employees and communities to create in the long-term an economy that serves all Americans.[9]

This statement and its position have been misconstrued by some to put forward stakeholder capitalism as a "theory that firms should be accountable to their stakeholders instead of their shareholders. Meaning, instead of serving their owners and being accountable to them, they should cater to the desires of the nebulous 'society.'"[10] This statement is false in that the definition of the Business Roundtable calls for serving all stakeholders, not one over the other, and declares doing so ultimately positions companies for long-term strength and success alongside their stakeholders.[11]

To ensure an organization's long-term success, pursuing purposeful behavior is the best practice for managing stakeholder value inside its stakeholder world. Purposeful behavior means taking actions that are consistent or aligned with a purpose that is meaningful and important to all the organization's stakeholders.[12] Traditionalists in business, according to Dr. Raj Sisodia and his two co-authors of *Firms of Endearment,* believe that broadening a company's concern to encompass all stakeholders can only be accomplished with a cost to shareholders. They claim this dilutes corporate focus on profit making and reduces it below their optimum levels. The error in this judgment draws from "either/or and if/then" limiting modes of thinking, which often narrows options to as few as two. By studying many firms and identifying 28 which they call "firms of endearment," the authors found them to be run by CEOs who are able to chart their companies' direction in the more inclusive terms of both/and thinking, which can yield virtually limitless options.[13]

It turns out that, when led and operated like the 28 companies Sisodia et al. found (including Whole Foods, Wegmans, and Commerce Bank), the group outperformed the S&P 500 by very impressive margins over 10-, 5- and 3-year time horizons, with returns of 1,026% for investors over the 10 years ending June 20, 2006, compared to 122% for the S&P 500, which is an 8:1 ratio.[14] "Endearing behavior by a company toward its stakeholders is one of the most decisive competitive differences ever wielded in capitalistic enterprise," and a growing number of companies are not content to confine their purpose just to lawful profitmaking.[15]

The underlying message threaded throughout this book and especially this chapter is, "why not reach for the stars and your highest potential and impact?" A place to start is the very structure of your business plan.

Your Beautiful Business, Intelligently Designed

While a riveted focus to serve your ecosystem of stakeholders provides a firm foundation, there is yet another level of conscious creation and execution available. Taking a cue from Steven Morris, an artist, business brand consultant, and author,[16] you are hereby invited

> into a way of doing business, a way of playing the game of business with beauty, integrity, belonging, magnetism, and love at its core... Part of beauty is that it's shaped with and by imperfections in its striving to be more beautiful. There's beauty in the striving... You won't always get exactly what you want, but maybe you'll get more than you bargained for.[17]

In addition to putting your company's purpose to work, Morris advocates taking agency of your evolution. That means, you must steward your own consciousness journey, mindfully and with continuous focus and effort. Other principles include allowing love to show up in your business and activating your magnetism as a company. Morris says, and I agree, that "it's a mistake, if not simply selling ourselves short, to leave *soul* out of our conversations around business. The invisible forces that animate us and bond us are worthy of direct infusion into the discussion and practices of our work."[18] Becoming present to this animating force is essential to finding and unleashing your gumption, with some ways to do so discussed in Chapter 8, Wake the Soul.

Morris and I share a lot of common perspectives on the enlivening and enlarging personal aspects for leaders when they reach for a more elevated, "beautiful" way of doing business. The beauty is both in the striving for such and the positive impact you can register when you actively architect a "beautiful" business. Morris and I are both devoted to nurturing leaders who have a sense of and are interested in stewarding their businesses to be more impactful and exponentially more valuable. He and I talked on air[19] about the principles of his book and our common missions to elevate leadership and business through consciousness and the cultivation of higher values.

This chapter on gumption is intentionally positioned first because I know from my research and working with clients that you, the leader who champions your organization, need hope, inspiration, and an infusion of energy and courage to take on today's business challenges and help your organization thrive. Morris extends this invitation to us all:

It is intended to be a revolution of our highest values. It is both about the morality of business and the values inherent within the beautiful struggle to create something that has lasting value and makes the world a better place. This is a call to awaken to a world of possibility in business. It is the antidote to disconnection, disintegration, and disengagement. This is a remedy to greed, gluttony, injustice, and pride. Make no mistake: the people of our world need this now. In Western culture, people are voting with their values and wallets and taking to the streets. The people that work within organizations are seeking to belong and contribute to something that matters.[20]

In choosing the path of the beautiful business, you will be rewarded with a purpose-filled life and business. Doing so occurs through an irresistible magnetism emanating from your beautiful business that will call forth the best of the people already in it and attract others outside who seek a more fulfilling way to live and work.

Dr. Ranjay Gulati's brilliant book, *Deep Purpose: The Heart and Soul of High-Performance Companies,* marries the beautiful business concepts Morris espouses with conscious and stakeholder capitalism through the lens of what he calls "deep purpose," which will be discussed in Chapter 5 – Ownership Culture that Unites All Stakeholders Through Purpose. Dr. Gulati and his team at Harvard have researched 18 high-performance companies and found they operate with heightened passion, urgency, and clarity. They thrive financially and organizationally while unleashing their full potential as a force for good. Your company, too, can come to represent humanity's best hope, leaving a lasting legacy for future generations.[21] You will hear more about Dr. Gulati and his message later in Chapters 5 and 8, but for now, you'll see how managing your business over the long term helps build value for all stakeholders.

The Long Play in Business

Drawing on the Business Roundtable's focus on creating long-term value, this last section brings home the importance of keeping your eye on making decisions and operating from your core purpose over the long haul to create the biggest value for all stakeholders. Corporate "short-termism" is killing a robust, resilient, and purpose-driven future. Companies are governed by the quarterly profit reporting system that encourages short-term, smaller-value results. The opportunity is to help companies and their leadership to develop smarter, more strategic financial incentives, instilling an ownership culture among employees to take actions that materially increase long-term value by linking strategy and execution to the core drivers of total shareholder returns. It takes courage to swim against the tide and play the long game.

Gregory Milano is founder and CEO of Fortuna Advisors, a thought leader and trusted advisor in helping clients transform their value creation potential through bold improvements to managerial insights, decisions, and behaviors. Milano is a recognized industry leader in financial performance measurement and valuation, capital allocation and incentive compensation. He is the author of *Curing Corporate Short-Termism: Future Growth vs. Current Earnings,* which we discussed on the *Working on Purpose* program.[22]

One of the biggest obstacles to economic growth, employment expansion, financial security, and social well-being is that companies are investing less and less in building their future and instead are devoting more and more capital to activities that provide a quick fix but deliver few, if any, lasting benefits.[23] Short-termism begins with and is largely governed by the quarterly earnings cycle. The problem is not that quarterly reporting is bad, but that the process that has been built up around these quarterly reports is fraught with demands and pressures that tend to influence management to over-emphasize short-term profitability results at the expense of the long-term growth and impact of the organization.

Milano says that almost everyone is aware of the problem, yet few business leaders know how to create an organizational environment with adequate accountability for delivering short-term results *without* sacrificing the long-term potential of the business. The quarterly earnings ritual has taken on increasing importance for public company leaders, and in many cases this triggers decisions that end up limiting success over the longer term. Executives tend to fear that their share prices will be crushed if they don't deliver earnings per share, or EPS, that meet or exceed analysts' consensus estimates.[24]

I was shocked to learn that, "When surveying over 400 chief financial officers, [the authors] found that some 80% of those CFOs expressed their willingness to sacrifice shareholder value simply to meet or beat a quarterly earnings goal."[25] Further: "In some companies, things are so bad that the people preparing the plan *know* it has no meaning; they are just compiling data and preparing materials as part of a routine designed to check a box and take home a paycheck."[26] In an effort to remedy this short-term view, entrepreneur Eric Ries has launched the Long-Term Stock Exchange (LTSE), the first national securities exchange promoting a long-term focus for investors and companies. The creation of LTSE is designed to minimize the pressure to hit short-term targets and allows for stewardship that stakeholders and society demand. These and other powerful entities are giving voice to our stakeholders. The LTSE was founded in 2015 in San Francisco and as of 2021 had two companies listed: the software company Twilio which enables communication to customers, and Asana, a web and mobile work management platform.[27]

To reinforce this longer-term focus, Milano advocates that leaders seek to create an ownership culture in which managers throughout the organization participate, and assume responsibility for decisions, results, and consequences. When each manager and employee accept their business obligations as if they owned them, organizations create more value.[28] Companies that embrace an ownership culture to promote a balanced, long-term outlook will make better investments, will be more accountable for delivering desirable returns on those investments, and will create more value. They will be guided by what investors do, rather than what they say, and they will generate more cash flow, deliver higher returns, and see their share price rise faster than those at their peer companies. Most important, they will feel less concerned with what their share price is next week or next month, and more concerned about what their share price will be in the long run.[29] We will more fully address the importance of creating an ownership culture through purpose in Chapter 5 and then provide ways to cultivate it in Chapter 8.

In summary, refocusing on your company or business unit with fresh eyes and looking for what's right and what more you can do with and through your company can provide a vital source of energy that inspires your way forward. This activity is akin to putting your own oxygen mask on first as directed by the airline flight crews. That oxygen supply then vitalizes you and allows you to extend a lifeline to all your stakeholders and ignite their commitment and performance in support of your business. Seeking additional ways your company can serve the world or community is invigorating for you at the helm, and, when communicated to your stakeholders, enrolls their hearts and minds. Everyone wants to know they're part of an organization that is doing good in the world and one they can be proud of. Inventing strategies with a longer-term focus, rather than solely operating on meeting quarterly earnings and shareholder value, and aptly communicating it for buy-in from all stakeholders, requires skill and finesse. Taken together, your gumption will be sufficiently raised to take on the challenges ahead of you. The time is now, right now. Put on that oxygen mask. In the next chapter, you'll learn about the urgency of revitalizing your company or department and recognize that time may be speeding up faster than you're aware.

Key Points Summary

❖ Let your business breathe vital life back into you: look at your company, or the area you lead, with fresh eyes and seek its potential growth, expansion, or novelty. Doing so will infuse you with inspiration, a critical energizing agent to fortify your efforts going forward.

❖ Map out all your stakeholders and consider how you can even better serve each of these communities through a Conscious Capitalism lens. Is there a way to create more value for them and increase your relational connection to them?

❖ Make your business beautiful through an elevated, intelligent design: step back and look at your company from a higher level, seeking additional ways to serve all stakeholders to enlarge impact.

❖ Play the long game in business: develop a long-term strategy to realize your company or department's purpose. Communicate that vision to all stakeholders, especially the investors who must understand how a tradeoff in short-term earnings is worth the longer-term payoff that likely satisfies more stakeholders with greater positive impact.

2

U: Urgency – Wake Up and Turn Fast! (When and Where)

You've had a long and successful run in your business, perhaps decades. Countless victories have been accumulated, each celebrated and ushering in the next period of your company's remarkable journey. Clearly, you've been doing some things right. At the same time, the world continues its fervent pace onward, and you must keep learning, growing, and changing with its tide. As Albert Einstein said, "we cannot solve our problems with the same thinking that created them." Employees are leaving their current employers in droves. You feel that pain as the unemployment rate dipped as low as 6.2% as of January 2022 and your job openings remain vacant for months. The Great Resignation is wreaking havoc on productivity and rising labor cost for companies. A contributing factor for those wishing to look for a new job is that people report feeling disconnected from their company. They are not engaged emotionally with the organization and its products or services. Today's times call for drastic measures. Hard turn now. Wake up and shed your old ways of thinking and operating that no longer serve your stakeholders.

Change and growth, in people and organizations, rarely happen in times of peace, ease, or stasis. Rather, substantial growth and transformation are most frequently spurred by difficulty, tragedy, and chaos. COVID-19 has served as the "world's heart attack," as often quipped by friend and colleague Dr. Neha Sangwan, MD,[1] and has helped awaken people to consider what they want from their lives. In many ways, the upheaval of the pandemic, the racial injustice movement, economic recession, and the recent Russia-Ukraine political conflict have stirred significant tensions and given people pause to consider the quality of their lives and work. And there's no going back. We can't – and moreover, shouldn't *want* to – put the genie back in the bottle and cling to old ways of managing stakeholders.

All this upheaval and change translates to a critical new world you need to navigate as a leader: work and how it gets done is now in the hands of the workers. The workers have spoken and made their demands clear. They want meaningful work in a company that aligns with their own values, are less willing to sacrifice their mental health and well-being to do so, and won't soon release the autonomy of working from home they gained in the pandemic. Welcome to the employee-driven workplace, also known as the "workplace of the people." This chapter addresses some of the most critical aspects emerging in today's workforce landscape that have likely crept up as you worked hard over the last few years to keep your company going. Starting with a recognition of the sheer speed at which today's information-driven world requires constant improvement in leadership and operations to remain relevant, we then turn to the adamant demand for a work-life harmony that allows people to center their work around their lives. The need to put mental health and well-being at the forefront of the company agenda and the need for autonomy in the choice of where work gets done are laid out as critical imperatives in today's times.

From Autopilot to a Constant Drive for Improvement

The urgency to radically shift to meet today's workforce requirements is incredibly sobering for many leaders, something Deborah Westphal and I discussed in our on-air conversation.[2] She said:

> For those entrenched or traditional business leaders, I hope you come away motivated to lead urgent and necessary change. Your experience and expertise are needed for making a vital shift within your organization, but radical change is required. Fifty years ago, the life expectancy of a Fortune 500 company was approximately seventy-five years. Now it is less than fifteen. This challenging, changing environment demands new ways of thinking about business and new mental models for leading effectively.[3]

The need to quickly discern what to keep and what to improve or discard in your business has never been greater. Huge quantities of information, constantly available and being served, presents a major challenge. Let these sobering statistics Westphal cites sink in:

> Today on average, human knowledge doubles every thirteen months. Because learning progresses in a nonlinear, cross-discipline manner, it's possible to segment the growth rates of specific industries and environments. For example, we know that technical knowledge and genetic information double every eighteen months. Knowledge that is related to online information doubles every six months. The knowledge base gained via social media networks doubles every twelve hours. How much of this knowledge is useful? How much is obsolete or just plain false?[4]

This sheer amount of new information constantly bombarding you and your business is a big reason behind writing this book – I am out to help you make sense of what is otherwise a head-spinning, confusing quandary. Rarely do organizations deliberately consider whether or what to discard or keep. They just layer new ideas into the existing decision-making framework. The result, like a packed closet, is a frustrating, even paralyzing, overabundance of choice.[5] Westphal coined the new term "obsoledge" to describe the phenomenon and says,

> Without intentionally working to set a vision and "tidy up," many of us fall into a habit of holding tight to outmoded approaches and operations. We are burdened by beliefs, behaviors, procedures, structures, and cultural artifacts that no longer serve a purpose. The remnants hinder progress, create confusion and conflict, and get in the way of achieving our organizational goals. Clearing the clutter positions our organizations to maneuver successfully through chaotic, fast-paced disruption to the point of resilience and fulfilled purpose.[6]

The ideas born out of a history of oversight, regulation, and constraint need to be pulled up from the root to free the organization of its "we can't do that" or "we do it this way" mentality that blocks progress with bias, risk aversion, and even misinterpretation. The tendency to fall victim to "obsoledge" has massive negative ramifications in your human capital practices. The tidying up process begins by identifying ideas that do not serve your business's purpose(s) and the obsoledge that exists across the organization. As facts, data, beliefs, and biases lose relevance, they gain the ability to inhibit growth and innovation. When many "best practice" business concepts sweep through companies like wildfire, they can tamp creative thinking. I'm willing to bet your company, like most, can benefit from taking stock of all operational policies and procedures, especially those touching your employees.

The Cry for Work-Life Harmony

Organizational Psychologist and Professor Anthony Klotz of Texas A&M predicted the Great Resignation as the pandemic was just setting in. Klotz declared that the pandemic and the way we went to work within it would point out the "unnatural aspects" of work, including long commutes to an office each day and lunch at a single prescribed time of the work day.[7] Klotz, as cited in an article in *Financial Review*, attributes the causes of the Great Resignation to pent-up interest to change jobs during the uncertainty of the initial pandemic days, evaluating meaning and contentment in the face of sickness or death during the pandemic, and a desire to move away from arranging one's whole life around work, and instead arranging work around life.[8] Before the pandemic struck, Buckingham and Goodall declared the need for companies to shed their centralized, bureaucratic ways that favor and feed the organization's need for efficiency and expediency at the expense of the workforce's heart, soul, and individuality.[9]

When you consider what has happened in the last few years, you can better understand and appreciate the seismic shifts that have occurred across many domains. In many ways, the world's consciousness has been "kicked upstairs" in response to the earth shaking beneath our collective feet during the COVID pandemic that began in March 2020 and continues today (as of this book's writing). People all over the world saw their lives turned completely upside down, as their cities ground to a halt during sheltering-in-place. It was as if the world was holding one large collective breath, waiting for this strange phenomenon to pass, so we could all just get on with our usual lives. But that's not what happened.

At all. Weeks turned to months, months to a year, now two. And still counting.

That forced halt to everyday life gave many people what those seeking enlightenment try to attain in their everyday life – silence. Silence, and the according "lack of noise" that comes along with it, can be absolutely deafening. With this "lack of noise," people start to hear, often for the first time, what their otherwise frenetic lives have been desperately trying to whisper to them. That whisper proves almost impossible to detect as people *run* to get groceries to make meals, *run* to get the kids off to school, *run* to drop in and check in on extended family needing care, and *run* to get to work. The hamster wheel of life stopped turning its dizzying pace during the early stages of the pandemic, which allowed those on it, at least for a moment, to step off and see what the world looked like when it wasn't constantly spinning around them.

As people obeyed the sheltering-in-place mandates and stayed away from public gatherings, many opting to pick up pre-ordered groceries or have them delivered, many found themselves looking at the beings inhabiting their home in ways they hadn't done prior to the shut in. People working from home suddenly, overnight, had the opportunity to eat lunch and dinner with their families for the first time in years. Or, perhaps, ever. They took walks together to get fresh air and sunshine. From my own front window perch on a quiet Dallas street, I witnessed whole families making their way down our tree-lined lane. The kids on scooters or bicycles, the adults slowly strolling alongside, sipping a beverage, and gaily conversing with those in the group. Moving caravans of reconnection. Of being *together* at a time when the world was coming undone.

The solace and solidarity that formed in the pandemic will likely forge lasting identities for everyone. Just as people can recall where they were when President J. F. Kennedy was killed or when the first plane hit the towers in New York City on 9/11, people today can remember where they were when they found out COVID had brought life to a standstill (I was driving from Dallas to Austin to spend spring break with my daughter when I heard the radio announcement that Dallas was shutting down that evening, so turned back home). They will also recall the people with whom they spent time during the pandemic and realize the outbreak's defining nature that altered the course of their lives. The forced rejoining of families and loved ones is something few people want to give up. Many of the leaders I work with told me wistfully of how their return to working in the office halted those precious reunions with spouses, children, family, and friends. The yearning for human connection and relationship is real and is one of five measures Dr. Martin Seligman has identified for well-being.[10] Ironically, the pandemic gave people the opportunity to experience and evaluate their key relationships. For a vast number, that evaluation process helped inform the decision to leave jobs requiring long commutes taking valuable time from loved ones, or hazardous work that could not be justified for the paycheck earned.

In the early months of the pandemic, as shocking numbers of people became sick with the virus and were hospitalized, the fleeting and precious nature of life rose to an elevated level of consciousness. Especially prior to the vaccine roll out, people witnessed those they loved or had worked with get sick and many die. Sickness and death are enormous wake-up calls for people. COVID in many ways has served as the world's shared galvanizing call. Facing down death for yourself or a loved one has a crisp way of helping you identify priorities and gain a clear line of sight to what you want your life to mean and stand for. When you lose someone you love, it offers you the chance to reevaluate how you've lived your life, the choices you've made so far, and how you want to live the rest of your life.

Brandon Peele, who I consider to be a brilliant and sentient human being, has taught me a lot about the opportunity for enlightened living and doing business. He's been a guest on the *Working on Purpose* program,[11] where we talked about his book, *Planet on Purpose*, in which he writes,

> We need a rapid awakening of every member of our species to discover our individual life's purpose AND, within the context of this global awareness and the emerging purpose of humanity, a purposeful reformation of our institutions and sovereign nations. In so doing, we answer the twin calls of purpose: (1) to discover and live what brings us most alive, and (2) from a sober understanding of reality, to listen to the call of what humanity, our ecology, the unborn, and the Cosmos are asking us to do to survive, thrive, and evolve.[12]

It is clear to me that the moment of awakening and recognition of the need to evolve in company operations has arrived.

This wake-up call, or what Professor Klotz refers to as "pandemic epiphanies," translates to a higher consciousness threaded among citizens across the globe.[13] Many people were able to transcend membership among the "walking dead," a phrase I reference and a group I aimed to awaken in my book *Purpose Ignited: How Inspiring Leaders Unleash Passion and Elevate Cause*.[14] The alarm clock has sounded and people across the world have woken to a new day. A great number of people, some sources say as much as half the North American workforce, planned to change jobs in 2021 and 2022. The eerie silence brought on by the pandemic, reconnection with people important in life, and the loss of those we know are powerful forces undergirding today's Great Resignation. People wanted some kind of change in all the discomfort of a life that felt for many to be out of their control – the world spinning around with no end in sight. Choice and change go hand in hand, with alarming numbers of people in the workforce choosing to vote with their feet and find a workplace more aligned with their wants, needs, and values. They are fleeing in masses and in doing so illustrate to others that opportunity exists elsewhere for them, too. As Dr. Gulati said so eloquently in our on-air conversation, "COVID has helped people want more from their lives,"[15] including work-life harmony and a focus on improving their mental health and well-being.

The Call for Well-Being Amid a Mental Health Crisis

As the pandemic continued to rage on, it became abundantly clear to many leaders that acknowledging the mental health crisis and addressing well-being in the workplace were paramount. The accumulation of stress, anxiety and fatigue were exacerbated and reverberated across companies. Those deemed "essential workers" heroically carried on their work in factories, hospitals, offices, and fields. Doing so put them in harm's way of a deadly virus no one understood in terms of behavior, mutation, and persistence. Burnout has emerged as a critical issue among today's workforce and requires an immediate posture that champions well-being across the spectrum of physical, social, emotional, spiritual, financial, environmental, and occupational needs.

Employees worked incredibly long hours trying to cover the demand for their services and the shortage of labor, and their physical and social health suffered in the effort and from reduced connection to loved ones. Those who work best in an office or desire strong social connection at work shriveled in the shut-out experience required by governments and chosen by companies. Healthcare workers on the front line reported utter exhaustion and burnout. Employees reported feeling disconnected from their employers and each other. Mental health and well-being plummeted for people working from home and in their workplaces.

Many leaders, perhaps yourself included, became more empathetic to their team members and their circumstances than ever before. While tensions between work and home have registered for decades, what was lacking was the power to do much about addressing and reducing these tensions. What has changed is that, during lockdown, leaders experienced these tensions firsthand. Thanks to a variety of quarantines, lockdowns, and work-from-home orders, leaders began to experience more viscerally the stresses and strains that so many other layers of the workforce constantly experience. For many leaders, the front-line experience has engendered a sense of understanding and empathy they'd previously lacked.[16] The result is that leaders have shed their "veil of ignorance"[17] and are now more motivated to put their shoulders to the wheels of quick wins and long-term changes to both immediately address and preserve the well-being of their workforce and steward a stronger future for their organizations.

Burnout is also gravely impacting productivity inside organizations[18] and has been cited as one of the key reasons employees are actively participating in the Great Resignation, quitting their current job before they even have another in hand.[19] So critical is the need to address and improve well-being in the workplace that Gallup, well known for its focus on measuring and improving employee engagement, pivoted to address well-being during the pandemic. Clifton and Harter, two of Gallup's highest-level professionals, published a book called *Wellbeing at Work: How to Build Resilient and Thriving Teams* in 2021.[20] Well-being is now a critical business driver requiring attention and resources. The "workplace of the people" has been described as a democratization of the workplace in terms of diversity, well-being, and work-life balance.

How this translates to running your business is that today's workforce prizes health, which means they want to exercise most days, eat healthy foods, and sleep eight hours per night. They also want time to give to friends, family, and their community. What this means for redesigning work is that companies that give their workforce sufficient autonomy over their schedules to take care of their health and relationships will attract more talent and keep them longer.[21] We'll address autonomy in various ways in the sections below. One other area that positively impacts and improves well-being is purpose, something Ray White and I discussed on air[22] and which will be discussed in detail in Chapters 5 and 8.

Fluid Location and the New Focus on Where Work Gets Done

Since people are re-evaluating their work requirements and looking for more flexibility to spend time nurturing relation-ships, having work-life harmony, and enjoying outside inter-ests,[23] providing autonomy to your team members and ways to manage their work around their lives is an employer differ-entiator. Another critical factor to evaluate is where, and even when, work gets done. That requires a focus on performance *outcomes*, as opposed to the antiquated eye on *presenteeism*.[24]

Consider some benefits of remote or hybrid work from both the vantage points of operational efficiency and productivity and enhancing the human experience of work, which I learned from Catherine Mattiske's *Leading Virtual Teams*[25] and our on-air conversation. From an economic perspective, it makes sound business sense for many companies to take a decentralized approach to organizational structures and consider moving away from the investment in acquiring or renting and maintaining work or office space. There are also benefits of geographical diversity; with employees worldwide who are natives of those countries or speak the local language fluently, your company gains a keen competitive edge in those countries, over single-country-based competitors. If you're trying to get a new product or service to market, you may find it quicker when leveraging the knowledge and connections of employees in different geographies with local people on your team who understand the political, financial, and corporate landscape. Pressures of the global marketplace and economy have increased the need for virtual management. Even though conducting international business has become technologically accessible, new strains have emerged when working with cross-cultural teams and the need to understand and overcome cultural and language difficulties.[26] You'll learn more about Mattiske's work and how to apply it in your organization in Chapter 6, Nurturing Through Mindfulness.

From the view of your team members, a curious realization happened for many people as they worked remotely, often for the first time – they came to understand they no longer needed to be physically bound or geographically close to the company they worked for. They could quite literally live anywhere, as long as they had a good internet connection. The exodus from the large, crowded cities sent many people to live near loved ones or in quieter, less populated areas.

Working remotely allows people to lose the commute time to the workplace and repurpose it toward other important activities in the day, including time with loved ones, exercise, or recreation. One thing is clear: a great number of people in the workforce do not want to surrender this newly found benefit ushered in by the pandemic – the flexibility of working from home. Meanwhile, employers want the control of having employees in the office where they can "see" them and monitor their work activities, with some outright admitting they do not trust their employees to be productive while working from home. Others tout the loss of innovation and connection registered when team members lose physical proximity to each other. Be that as it may, today's "workforce of the people" has tasted freedom and is highly resistant to giving it up. Sources vary in reporting the percentage of the workplace desiring at least a hybrid environment, with one at

45%[27] and a current client reporting 70% of their workforce. Health benefits to team members include a greater ability to focus, reduced travel time, and increased family connection.[28]

Whether you offer remote or a hybrid approach to working from home and office, the demand for flexibility in where work gets done is here to stay. Finding the optimum fit for your company's operations and the individual interests of your team members is key. Companies that consider their interests to be more important than those of the people powering them risk alienating their very lifeblood. An immediate halt to traditional operational practices that require 100% adherence to an on-site work policy is necessary to remain a competitive contender attracting talent to your business.

Key Points Summary

❖ Go off autopilot and examine all your business practices, especially as they relate to your workforce. The more quickly you replace outdated practices that alienate your people, the faster you can get back on track to thriving.

❖ Your workforce now wants more from you than steady work and a paycheck. They are voting with their feet for meaning and work-life harmony. You can stop them at the door when you listen and create a work environment they increasingly demand.

❖ It is critical you assess and address well-being in your workplace. Burnout is real across all levels in your company. The sooner you recognize and put measures in place to elevate well-being, the sooner you're back on track to thrive.

❖ People want a meaningful life and will no longer tolerate having to craft a life solely around work. Adding flexibility and autonomy to how work gets done at your company go a long way to help your employees live life on their terms.

❖ Seriously listen to where and when your workforce wants to work and consider how to provide that for them. Let go of your traditional focus on work getting done at the office or workplace within a certain schedule.

3

S: Sustainability in an Interdependent World (Why)

Twenty-six thousand, four hundred sixty-two, and a half. That's the average number of days you've got on the planet when you live to 72.5 years, which the average of 70 and 75, the global statistic for men and women, respectively.[1] The lifespan of the average business is about 10 years, or 3,650 days, also a good amount of time to make a meaningful impact on the greater world around you. Whatever your position on sustainability, the aim of this chapter is to expand your thinking on the matter to recognize that active stewardship of your sustainability is now not only requisite from a government standpoint but also makes your organization more enticing to your stakeholders.

By "sustainability," a simple way to understand the term is to consider how 9–10 billion people will live reasonably well with the constraints of one planet by mid-century (that is, 2050).[2] Actions to address sustainability issues to align with major global environmental goals by 2030 include specific temperature goals as outlined in the Paris Agreements and the UN Sustainability Goals. Specifically, those goals are to keep global temperature rise this century well below 2 degrees Celsius above pre-industrial levels and, better still, to limit the temperature increase even further to 1.5 degrees Celsius.[3]

It helps to embrace system thinking, which automatically aids in understanding the various components within and see relational interactions. You live in a wondrous, magical system called the world. Its beauty and wonder can literally take your breath away. So can careless, thoughtless actions… take your breath away. Literally. Your daily actions have consequences, for better or worse. Do you let the water continue to run as you brush your teeth, or shut it off until you're ready to rinse your mouth? Do you recycle paper, plastics, and other items? Do you intentionally refill water in a favorite cup or do you daily turn toward your plastic bottle of water, only to discard it after it's empty? Multiply all those actions and many others by the number of people in your company or department and you will begin to realize the difference you can make to sustain the health of our planet. Wherever you are on the conservationist/sustainability spectrum, it is becoming increasingly difficult to ignore the health of the environment and the interdependence of all forms of life inhabiting the planet.

Beyond the obvious need for viability of humanity along with that of our fellow species, a sustainability focus is increasingly taking center stage in business. This chapter acquaints you with the idea that sustainability efforts have become an unignorable business imperative that moves from a consumption, ego-driven mindset toward a more "live and let live" attitude to steward health and vitality in an interdependent world. You'll learn how much more alive and alert your organization can become and how it must operate in the stakeholder capitalism world we are navigating. By recognizing you and your business have a role to play in improving your immediate ecosystem and beyond, your empowering invitation to elevate your business operations awaits. May this awakening and corresponding elevation of consciousness be like seeing a vision of a strong rope dangling invitingly from the sky, hooked to a universe beyond your comprehension, and beckoning you to climb. You and your business can do *so* much more than you have believed to make a positive contribution to sustainability through many measures and through your stakeholders. Today's populace now strongly demands you take firm actions and is holding companies to account accordingly by voting with their feet as employees and their pocketbooks as consumers.

On Becoming Wise Homo Sapiens

Much of this book is an invitation to elevate your consciousness and that of the team you lead – to become more fully and vibrantly aware. You are familiar with the Latin term "homo sapiens," which means "wise man," or how we humans not so humbly refer to ourselves.[4] You owe it to yourself, your team members, the success and longevity of your organization, and the planet to learn, understand, and adjust your individual and organizational collective behavior to walk as softly as you can on our planet Earth. Consider this alluring promise:

> We are in the process of realizing our self-given name as a species: *Homo sapiens sapiens* or the being that "knows that it knows." In becoming "doubly wise," we turn the knowing faculty back upon itself and, ultimately, become aware that we are awareness itself – an invisible knowing presence at the foundations of the living Universe.[5]

Increasingly, there is a preponderance of overlap in how various authors, subject matter experts, and film makers depict the stance that the universe as a whole is intelligent.[6] These authors and creators put forth the idea there is intelligence embedded and woven into the fabric of the universe. Moreover, the cosmos (or universe) is becoming increasingly self-aware through the evolution of life and the conscious structures within it that are uniquely and increasingly geared to connect with each other and express unique purpose.[7] Eco-awakening refers to what's calling us now – beyond psyche/soma/spirit – to understand how we're connected to the universal consciousness and can cooperate with evolution.[8]

If you are curious about or would like to extend your knowledge and connection to nature and humanity's interdependence with it, I highly recommend you see the documentary *My Octopus Teacher*.[9] At the time of writing, I have watched the Oscar-award winning film 11 times and continue gaining new insights with each viewing. So enthralled was I with the film that to me beautifully showcases all living beings' tender interdependence, I sought someone connected to the film to interview on the *Working on Purpose* radio program. Thanks to Ellie ter Haar, a newfound American friend living in New Zealand, I met via an online zoom session with Swati Thiyagarajan, the associate producer of the film and wife of its producer and narrator Craig Foster.

Thiyagarajan, a conservationist journalist, shares in her book *Born Wild*[10] a saying oft repeated to her in her childhood by her Uncle Siddharth, an ornithologist who taught her to love and respect all living things: "It is arrogant of us to imagine that we are killing this planet. With our lifestyles what we are doing is actually only killing our ability to survive on this planet. Nature will evolve beyond us," said Uncle Siddharth. "She will always survive because she learnt to adapt and grow, while we are still learning how to live."[11] In other words, we humans are not nearly as smart and in charge as we might like to think.

We have the opportunity to listen deeply to the call of what humanity, ecology, and the unborn are asking us in order to survive, thrive, elevate, and thus cooperate with evolution. Max Scheler goes so far as to say that the role of the human being in the cosmos is the infusion of life with spirit,[12] which seems to suggest we have available agency and a catalyzing glue. To know what it means to be human, we must understand what it means to be connected to and in service of the whole cosmos – and thus actually become wise.

Your "Living Organization" in Today's Stakeholder Capitalism World

Forget for a moment that earth is a tiny particle in the universe and turn your attention to your own "planet" – your business. Your organization has its own ecosystem. Complexity and interdependency are our reality, and our economic and business theories need to evolve to reflect this truth. It helps to view corporations as living beings that have within them, from their moment of creation, a "purpose for being" that wants to be realized. "The Living Organization," as coined by Norman Wolfe,[13] captures this evolutionary idea. The Living Organization wants to make its mark, fulfill its purpose, and maximize its contributions to the customers it serves. Living organisms, and organizations, are in relationship with their environment and full ecosystem which consists of all its stakeholders (customers, employees, investors, suppliers, and the community).[14] When organizations are viewed in this light, their members are better positioned to reach for a higher level of service within the ecosystem of stakeholders[15] and practice conscious capitalism principles to do business that intends to better the world.[16]

David Grayson and his two fellow authors stress the importance of business focusing on sustainability:

> Our sense is that if more businesses do not take more responsibility for their impacts and innovate to become more sustainable voluntarily, then a growing wave of populism and social unrest may compel governments to force changes on the private sector – especially if businesses and society do not prepare

effectively for the job losses coming from automation and the Fourth Industrial Revolution.[17]

Read that passage carefully. Among other things, its message is that capitalism is at risk when we ignore the needs of stakeholders and the increasing interest to steward sustainability. What is meant by corporate sustainability? It can be simply situated as "a company's delivery of long-term value in financial, environmental, social, and ethical terms," which aligns with the definition of the United Nations Global Compact.[18] Looking at the evolution of sustainability through the business lens, Grayson and team share what they view as the various eras in which the topic has been addressed: the harm reduction era, 1997–2005; strategic integration era, 2006–2015; and the purpose-driven era, 2016–ongoing. The trend forward is quite ambitious, with Grayson et al. seeing a fourth epoch of corporate sustainability leadership on the horizon, which they call the regenerative era. From 2025 onward, this era will find a critical mass of companies committing to a circular economy or closed-loop approach to business, as well as redesigning business models to optimize the economic, environmental, and social positives of all they do.[19] Thus, the authors emphasize the criticality of looking "at the scale and pace of change that economies, the environment, and society are experiencing through the lens of sustainability leadership, particularly the private sector's contribution to ameliorating the challenges facing the world today."[20] I support Simon Mainwaring's admonition that we should think of ourselves as "corporate ecologists" and that "We must acknowledge neutrality is complicity."[21]

From an "Ego Economy" to a "Living Economy"

Even while recognizing that humanity is part of a shared existence among all beings in the planetary system, you can still lack the breadth of vision and connection to truly understand your place in the system of systems. To control your present and shape your future requires a clarity about your relationship with all systems – other people, your community or industry, your society, your culture, and overall humanity, the largest human system of all.[22] Look further and step beyond your own species, and you'll gaze in wonder at the vast world that lies beyond. Duane Elgin, who has been speaking, consulting, researching, and writing on our time of "great transition" to a more regenerative future, states:

> [T]he most urgent challenge facing humanity is not climate change, or species extinction or unsustainable population growth; rather, it is how we understand the Universe and our intimate relationship within it. Our deepest choices for the future emerge from this core understanding.[23]

Elgin makes his point more directly by saying:

> [S]hort-term material prosperity is being gained at the cost of long-term ecological ruin. As Wendell Berry reminds us, nature "has more votes, a longer memory, and a sterner sense of justice than we do." We are creating by our own hand a long-term future that is unforgivingly inhospitable for advancing human civilization.[24]

And hang on, there's more sobering news to put things into clearer perspective. Elgin continues:

> More than 20 major civilizations have collapsed over the millennia, including the empires of the Romans, Mayans, Aztecs, Easter Islanders, Anasazi, Mesopotamians, and the Soviets. Importantly, many examples of collapse involve climate change as a key contributing factor. Although collapse has occurred

numerous times throughout history, today is different in one crucial respect: there are no frontiers left. *The circle has closed.* The entire world has become a single, integrated system – economically, ecologically, and socially.[25]

The COVID pandemic illustrated this "integrated system" convincingly. Almost overnight, or at least over a few months starting in the early months of 2020, the world's population could glimpse an inseparable connectedness. Many people across the world came to understand that we really are "in this together." What that means is that every person today must care for the planet, together. There is no opting out.

When our personal aliveness becomes transparent to the aliveness of the living Universe, transformational experiences of wonder and awe emerge naturally. As we open into the cosmic dimensions of our being, we feel more at home, less self-absorbed, more empathy for others, and an increased desire to be of service to life. These shifts in perspective are immensely valuable for building a sustainable future.[26]

When you recognize you are breathing the same air as someone across the farthest reaches of the world and swim in the same ocean of water,

[T]hen it is understandable that we each have some measure of direct experience of being in communion with the larger fabric of life. Because we share the same matrix of existence, the totality of life is already touching each of us and co-creating the field of aliveness within which we exist.[27]

This translates to how you can consider sustainable living – for yourself and your company.

In seeing the Universe as alive, we naturally shift our priorities from an "ego economy" based upon consuming deadness to a "living economy" based upon growing aliveness. An aliveness economy seeks to touch life more lightly while generating an abundance of meaning and satisfaction.[28]

If the ideas in this chapter aren't already uplifting enough as aspirational principles, there are numerous examples of companies stewarding actual inspiring sustainability journeys. We can look to the example of CEO Ray Anderson who, after a life-changing epiphany, set out on a high-stakes quest to eliminate all negative environmental impacts by 2020. The head of the global public company Interface, he completely turned this carpet tile manufacturer's focus from "plundering" the earth by using fiber that wasn't biodegradable toward one much more planet-friendly, as featured in the *Beyond Zero* documentary.[29] There has been a recent increase in the corporate world taking on the challenges of environmental sustainability, with large European companies in the vanguard. For example, Swedish global furniture giant IKEA powers most of its stores with solar energy, aiming not only to become electricity neutral, but ultimately to build a surplus of juice to share with local communities. We also see this commitment in IKEA's supply chain, where almost half its wood comes from sustainable foresters, and all its cotton from farms that meet the Better Cotton standards. Those are just a few of the many regenerative policies IKEA enacted by following a simple set of efficient, resourceful instructions toward "People and Planet Positive."[30]

Sustainability and ESG as a Business Imperative

The March 21, 2022 Securities Exchange Commission ruling that companies must disclose emissions is another step toward mandating sustainability practices; in other words it's become "everyday business."[31]

An unprecedented level of sensibility toward what is expected of business leaders on environmental, social, and governance (ESG) issues affecting companies has emerged. Now is the moment for businesses and brands to determine what they will stand for. Figuring out what you think about and will do on matters of social justice, inclusion, climate change, and pay equity can energize the positive forces of company character, helping your organization attract and retain loyal employee, customer and investor followings that strengthen communities. Doing so is not just good for the bottom line but also enlivens the overall ecosystem in which you operate.

The business agenda must now regard matters that were once the sole purview of global causes. Issues including the aging population, low birth rates, the dominance of the millennial demographic, hyper-segmentation, disenfranchised young people, loneliness, and depression have become part of the corporate agenda.[32] To fully operate from your organization's purpose, according to Ranjay Gulati, CEOs must become more comfortable speaking out as activists on key issues relating to their purpose. In fact, more executives have adopted activist postures in recent years, staking out positions on an array of social and environmental topics.[33] Leaders must strengthen their activism so that it comes across as genuine and meaningful.[34]

As Frank Calderoni says, company character is the core that grounds culture and strategy – it is the persistent through-line of fundamental beliefs and values uniting people and teams working with a shared purpose. Character comprises the qualities and behaviors that define us as people – such things as empathy, courage, authenticity, integrity, honesty, and respect. They are embodied in how we work every day, how we treat others, and how we treat ourselves. Organizations that internalize and live and demonstrate *upstanding company character* in every interaction are the organizations that will win today – and into the future.[35] Company character is the integrity, respect, and fortitude residing at the core of your culture. Your company's culture expresses your character, which can create tremendous competitive advantage. "People make decisions on what to buy, where to work, whom to partner with, and whom to affiliate with based on a company's values and on the character (or lack of it) displayed by its people."[36]

The combinations of a global pandemic, recession, and social justice movements are unlike anything we've experienced in our lifetime, and we're all dealing with the heightened expectations that employees, customers, and investors have of the business sector to lead the way through daily change. People are holding companies accountable for societal, environmental, and governance practices with little to no patience for inaction.[37] Customers and the workforce expect leaders to focus on profit as well as purpose and want their leaders to not only focus on ESG (environmental, social, governance) issues but also take a public stand on them.[38] Those who don't will find their employees opt out of employment or never apply for a job in the first place, and customers give purchase preference toward companies that align with their values and demonstrate ESG (environmental, social, and governance) commitments.[39]

Calderoni describes a brilliant example of the difference that can be made when a company takes a stand on social injustice. He shares how Coca-Cola's then chairman J. Paul Austin took a stand on the January 27, 1965 planned party to celebrate Dr. Martin Luther King's Nobel prize win (when at first no one was planning to attend). Austin assembled a group of business elite and said: "It is embarrassing for Coca-Cola to be located in a city that refuses to honor its Nobel prize winner. We are an international business. The Coca-Cola Company does not need Atlanta. You all have to decide whether Atlanta needs the Coca-Cola Company."[40] As a result of this speech, 1,500 tickets were immediately purchased to attend the dinner celebration. Now, that's making a difference in the world and putting your money where your mouth is.

Maybe this was just a different era? No, that's not it. Another thing Calderoni and I talked about on air was his experience recently joining a group of CEOs convened by Google. The discussion topic was the change in sensibility toward business leaders engaging on ESG issues directly and indirectly affecting their companies. The consensus?

> Engaging is no longer optional. Now is the moment for businesses and brands to figure out what they will stand for – which happens to also be a tenet of upstanding character. Figuring out what you think about and will do on matters of social justice, inclusion, climate change, or pay equity, for example, can energize the magnetic, positive forces of company character, helping your organization attract and retain loyal employee, customer, and investor followings that strengthen companies.[41]

Companies and their leaders can't be silent on racial justice or sustainability, as two examples. When we are silent on issues that matter, people will fill in the gaps themselves – and most likely negatively. If we don't convey and demonstrate our support for diversity and inclusion, then top candidates will pass us by – looking for employers that do. If we don't talk about our stance on climate change, they'll assume we don't care about climate change, when we actually do.[42] Sustainability has become a business imperative. In the next chapter, you'll learn about "therapy" readily available to you and your stakeholders to fortify your efforts requisite to play in today's world demanding meaning and purpose.

Key Points Summary

- ❖ Humans are not nearly as smart as they think they are, but the universe is. It will go on without its human occupants. Repositioning the stance on what's best for the planet and its sustainability starts with recognizing how short-lived humanity stands to become, absent sustainability interventions.

- ❖ Redirecting a focus away from "what's good for me" and my company or business to "what's good for all of us living on the planet" helps leaders make informed decisions and choices about using and disposing of resources.

- ❖ Sustainability is today's business imperative. Leaders must have a clear, compelling, and public plan of how they will steward their company toward their ESG goals.

- ❖ Business leaders today are called to take a public stand on ESG matters pertaining to their company values and character. Doing so aligns core stakeholders and energizes their committed affiliation, which translates to committed customers, loyal team members, and supportive affiliations to champion the company forward.

T: Therapy that Enlivens Hearts and Souls Through Meaning (How)

It is virtually impossible to experience a single day without hearing both "meaning" and "purpose" uttered somewhere throughout its course. So interwoven into today's vernacular are these words that they've become "green washed" and lost much of their energizing motivation and direction, respectively. Where the next chapter will focus on the matter of purpose, this chapter distinguishes the term "meaning" to otherwise provide core access to its vitalizing force. Specifically, from the vantage point of my education and practice as an organizational logotherapist, "meaning" is rendered in this chapter in what I hope you will find a delightfully simple manner that offers ways to open new realms of possibility that can energize all the stakeholders in your ecosystem by igniting their intrinsic motivation. First, the sheer fixation on the matter of meaning will help you understand why it's such a critical area to manage in your organization. Logotherapy is then introduced as a specific lever to activate the sources of energy that are available when meaning is discovered in the world of work. You'll learn how work offers one of the most fertile playgrounds through which to activate meaning for people and then become acquainted with the practice of "managing through meaning" to enliven you and your company in ways you never imagined.

The Workforce Hungers for Deep Meaning

With the elevation in consciousness described thus far in this book comes higher workforce demands. A stable job, decent pay and benefits, and opportunities for advancement are no longer sufficient to motivate and retain your people. Your team members want to know that spending precious time in their lives toiling for you matters and positively contributes to their overall lives. One of the driving forces propelling the Great Resignation is the search for more meaningful work.

A long list of indicators exists to illustrate how a lack of meaning translates to the quality of people's lives and the actions they take within them. Emily Esfahani Smith speaks of the "meaning crisis," which manifests as a rise in hopelessness and misery. The US rate of depression has risen dramatically since 1960, with the use of anti-depressants rising by 400% during the years 1988–2008, she reports. The World Health Organization (WHO) reports global suicide rates are up by 60% since World War II. In fact, writes Esfahani Smith, each year some 40,000 Americans take their lives; globally, that figure is 1 million. Astounding. Moreover, the wealthiest nations report higher happiness, lower meaning, and higher suicide rates than poor countries, and countries with the lowest rates of meaning register the highest suicide rates. She goes on to say that four in 10 Americans have not discovered a satisfying life purpose, and a quarter of Americans do not have a clear sense of what makes their lives meaningful.[1] "The search for meaning has become incredibly urgent and yet also elusive for so many."[2] I know from my own first-hand research and experience speaking to audiences that there is a good segment of the world who don't know what they're passionate about and are apathetically moving through life, a phenomenon I seek to ameliorate in *Purpose Ignited: How Inspiring Leaders Unleash Passion and Elevate Cause.*[3] There is a constant refrain that people want to live meaningful lives, to have meaningful work, and to enjoy meaningful relationships. But what does "meaning" actually mean? Meaning speaks to that which is significant to a person, what matters to them, what moves them. Meaning is registered in the limbic brain in the proximity of where memories and emotions are processed. In its simplest terms, meaning indicates the significance or value people place on their lives and the experiences they encounter in doing so.

Victor Frankl in *The Will to Meaning* says the main manifestations of a lack of meaning, experienced as existential frustration, are boredom and apathy,[4] which present in the organizational collective as disengagement, lackadaisical performance, and little to no innovation. The fast pace and rush of the work week can serve to mask the emptiness people feel in their lives and work, and Sunday can be the saddest day of the week for people. You have a golden opportunity in your organization to greatly lift people's lives through the work you offer them. As you'll learn in Chapter 7, Open the Heart, giving people the opportunity to do meaningful work eradicates the Sunday neurosis while lifting employee engagement, performance, and retention measures.

Enter Logotherapy: The Surprisingly Simple Path to Activate Meaning

For people to be fulfilled in life and for organizations to thrive, discovering and experiencing meaning in life and work is an existential and operational imperative. "When the way we're living doesn't align with what we consider important, it conflicts with our sense of self. That's what happens in disengagement."[5] A foundation on which to build a solution and a way forward rests in logotherapy.

Logotherapy, or "healing through meaning" in Greek, is a psychological and motivational theory developed by Dr. Viktor Frankl.[6] Based on his experience as a medical doctor, psychiatrist, neurologist, and philosophy student, Dr. Frankl formulated his meaning-centered approach. Its philosophical approach touts meaning as humankind's chief concern, promotes freedom of choice and personal responsibility, and it is now internationally recognized and practiced within a variety of segments. Frankl developed his theory while working to address and reduce suicides in teens and women in counseling centers and psychiatric hospitals in Vienna, Austria, in the 1930s. He developed his ideas about logotherapy before he entered the concentration camp as a Holocaust prisoner during World War II at the age of 37, where his encounters with the worst human conditions confirmed his theory – those prisoners who were oriented toward a meaning to be fulfilled were more likely to survive.

Since the birth of logotherapy as a psychological theory, Dr. Frankl went on to author over 30 books, with *Man's Search for Meaning*[7] registering incredible popularity and impact with millions of copies sold in dozens of languages. The Viktor Frankl Institute offers courses and an advanced degree in Logo-Philosophy, which I have completed and have since incorporated the principles and learning into my work[8] and why I refer to myself as an Organizational Logotherapist.[9] Increasingly, logotherapy is being leveraged in Education, Business, and Nation Building, to name just a few. Two early pioneers in the field are the married duo Dr. Alex Pattakos and Elaine Dundon, who have authored books on the topic of meaning[10] and founded the Global Meaning Institute,[11] where they work with many entities to help leaders cultivate meaning in their organizations. Specifically, they incorporate their discipline called MEANINGology® to advance the human quest for meaning in life, work, and society. They are just one shining example of how logotherapy is gaining traction to help ameliorate the "crisis of meaning" impacting so much of the world.

To better understand logotherapy, it's helpful to recognize that it "finds its philosophical roots in existentialism and phenomenology, its psychological roots in psychoanalysis and individual psychology, and its spiritual roots in a profound commitment to the human being as an irreducibly spiritual creature."[12] Logotherapy offers a simple set of practices to discovering meaning anytime, anywhere, for anyone. My attraction to logotherapy and its application into my management consulting practices is due to its optimistic approach to life, its focus on well-being, and its position that everyone has a treasure-trove of spiritual resources readily available to deal with life's most difficult challenges while appreciating with awe its greatest gifts. To apply logotherapy in your organization is to activate intrinsic motivation in your workforce – to literally turn your people on from the inside out and give them radiant health and well-being. Logotherapy, applied in organizations, can be seen as a way to "vitalize through meaning" all stakeholders connected to your business or organization. Concerned with a person's aspirations and frustrations, logotherapy is based on three concepts: the freedom of will, the will to meaning, and the meaning of life.[13]

Logotherapy is a philosophy, motivational theory, and application of psychology that is based on three core assumptions:

- Life has meaning under all circumstances, even the most miserable ones.
- Humankind's main motivation for living is the will to find meaning in life.
- People have the freedom to find meaning in what they do and what they experience, or at least in the stand they take when faced with a situation of unchangeable suffering.[14]

Those three simple premises underlying logotherapy can be used to address and ameliorate the existential vacuum, that deep vat of misery experienced when people cannot discern meaning or reach toward meaningful goals.

Meaning is registered through a person's value system. In other words, what is meaningful to one person may not register as such at all to another, because their values differ. As I shared in my first book, *Purpose Ignited*,[15] logotherapy and the Franklian psychology that informs it hold there are three principal ways of finding meaning, both in the moment and as ultimate meaning in life, as follows:

- Creative: what you give to the world in terms of creations.
- Experiential: what you take from the world in the way of encounters or experiences.
- Attitudinal: the stand you take to all predicaments when you face a fate you cannot change.

I have come to associate these ways of discovering meaning with more common words used in today's parlance, like this:

- Creative = PASSION
- Experiential = INSPIRATION
- Attitudinal = MINDSET

According to logotherapy, happiness is a byproduct of finding meanings.

Logotherapy maintains and restores mental health by providing a sound view of the human being and the world as we know it. It draws on the huge reservoir of health stored in our specifically human dimension – our creativity, our capacity to love, our reaching out to others, our desire to be useful, our ability to orient to goals, and our will to meaning. Logotherapy emphasizes what is right with us, what we like about ourselves, our accomplishments, and our peak experiences. It also considers the qualities we dislike so we may change them, our failures so we can learn from them, our abysses so we may lift ourselves up, knowing that peaks exist and can be reached.[16]

Logotherapy focuses on meanings yet to be fulfilled and thus is meaning-centered psychotherapy. Logotherapy looks for strengths that could be activated and brought to bear in any existential situation. While acknowledging present difficulties, it looks to the future with hope, trusting that inner resources are available which can be tapped.[17] As viewed through logotherapy, "the vitality of a person's life at every stage depends upon his or her supply of meaning."[18]

Thus, embracing a logotherapeutic culture stimulates human agency and the capacity to persist and take self-responsibility among all stakeholders. This encourages people to take the initiative for themselves in the workplace, an idea that ought to be refreshing to many leaders who can otherwise feel the weight of their team members' expectation to ignite their engagement. In reality, only individuals themselves have the optimal capacity to do so. You have a tremendous opportunity to awaken your team members to their own meaning through everyday experiences they have at work, which will be discussed in more detail in Chapter 7, Open the Heart. When you help people discover and experience more of the meaning they crave, you enable them to activate and unleash an abundance of intrinsic motivation and energy, exactly what you need to power engagement and performance in your organization.

The Playground of Work – Where Meaning is Delightfully Activated

The global meaning crisis that is draining the life out of people and the organizations that employ them can be radically improved by applying logotherapeutic principles into organizational leadership and culture. The hunger for meaningful connection with others, a life and work of purpose, and to enjoy a bigger, more beautiful life is palpable and helps explain the unrest as people move from job to job. Of course, some people don't know what they're looking for, or running from. But there are many others, committed people who want to be in an organization where they can forge deep relationships while expanding their potentials. They want to be part of building something that matters, with people who share their passion. They also want to grow and differentiate themselves as unique and special.

Logotherapy postulates that people are at their best with a certain healthy tension. We are well advised to avoid physical and psychological tensions, but logotherapy regards the tension of the spirit reaching toward potential as healthy. A healthy state results from stretching from what we are to what we have the vision of becoming,[19] which can also be termed personal and professional growth. In fact, meaning can be discovered through constant striving toward a new self that is closer to your potential than your present self and through constant attempts to interrelate with others. The logotherapeutic approach consists of widening and broadening the visual field of a person so that the whole spectrum of potential meaning becomes conscious and visible to him or her.[20] You will learn how you can fold logotherapeutic principles into your culture and operations to vitalize your team members and all stakeholders in Chapter 7, Open the Heart.

Frankl says, "This human capacity to find meaning in unique situations is conscience. Thus, education must equip [people] with the means to find meanings."[21] Organizations have a tremendous opportunity to equip their people with this education and thereby activate the powerful force of meaning throughout its ecosystem. By nurturing and stewarding the path to meaning and purpose, companies position themselves for a compelling future with vibrant relationships with all their stakeholders, elevating their consciousness along the way. The more individuals become aware of their interconnections to others within and across the company, and then increasingly reach through their communities and ecosystems, the more conscious their actions and greater the increase in their energy and efforts.

People spend more than a third of their lives at work. This dimension of life offers people a very effective way to quell the spiritual malaise mentioned earlier when a life otherwise devoid of meaning shows its insignificance on Sunday or when the rush of the week calms down. Specifically, logotherapy rests on a premise that people realize optimal vitality when serving other people, also known as self-transcendence,[22] which has the magnificent added by-product of happiness. You and your team have a tremendous opportunity to be of service to others through the work you do each day. Communicating this through your culture and leadership is essential to creating a meaning-fortified energy force in your company.

Work and the meaning it registers for people has often been considered from the individual vantage point. Yet so much of work occurs in the context with others and so is socially constructed. That is, we draw upon social cues from people through culture, symbols, and the like when making sense of what is meaningful. "Because work is often conducted in socially rich contexts, organizations are in a unique position to help members cultivate and enact meaningful work."[23] Organizations have a tremendous opportunity to influence how people see themselves and to position meaning and purpose for their constituents to make them both delightfully accessible and thereby energized, providing them a wonderful playground in which to realize their highest potential.

Doctor's Orders: Motivate Through Meaning

Your people ache to know they matter, that you notice and appreciate their efforts to fulfill their work and make their contribution. You must first anchor your organization in meaning through your leadership and cultural practices. The next step is to cascade that learning to your managers who can then help their direct reports find meaning in their everyday tasks.[24] By teaching each of your team members to access meaning for themselves, you empower them to activate their intrinsic motivation and flourish. Doing so takes managerial prowess and ultimately transfers the burden of employee engagement from the manager to the team member, where it ultimately belongs and is best enabled.[25] The key is for managers to create environments where meaning is constantly accessible.

People want to be part of something that matters, and they revel in knowing they had a part in helping build an organization of impact. There is so much managers can do to humanize the workplace, inviting their team members to "suck the marrow of life" through their everyday work experiences.

Organizations are well served to move away from the strong tendency to use extrinsic motivators like pay and benefits to encourage impassioned performance and a devoted stay and to incorporate intrinsic motivators informed through meaning and logotherapy.[26] Today, the leader's number one job is to champion meaning in the organization, which will drive engagement and resilience, health and well-being, and performance and innovation to higher levels.[27] One of the best ways to experience meaning is to be near the people you help.[28]

Organizations can't give meaning, they can only create an environment in which individuals can be their own prime movers in a meaning process. This process can't be managed and measured like the logical processes [in other operational aspects] and needs its own metrics – one of which is the success of the company.[29]

Rather, a "more appropriate model for today may be Peter Senge's Learning Organization, which demands that everyone strive for the level of personal introspection, responsibility, and ownership that self-actualizing people tend to exhibit."[30]

Employees must be able to see the connection between what they find meaningful and the work they do for the organization. There's usually a connection; people end up in jobs for a reason. But it's incumbent on organizations to create environments that help employees make the connection. The success of the organization and the individual both depend on it. Lack of engagement is the symptom [of lack of performance], not the disease.[31]

Companies can't motivate workers intrinsically – forging powerful, emotional connections between employees, their work, and their employers – merely by setting ambitious strategic goals. They must also draw on their inherent human need to elevate themselves by contributing to something bigger or transcendent. According to a psychology theory Ranjay Gulati discusses called the meaning maintenance model,

[W]e all seek meaning or purpose in our lives as human beings. We look to meaning to understand our relationship with others, we make meaning ourselves, and we quickly seek out new forms of meaning when our ways of seeing the world come under attack.[32]

When organizations can help their team members access greater meaning in their lives and work, all boats rise as the individual becomes more fortified and motivated, their passion and energy increases, and they are mobilized to contribute at a higher level of their talent and purpose. Companies are well served to invest in educating their workforce from this logotherapeutic foundation because doing so activates a self-directing and self-vitalizing force from within, which then empowers the individual while fortifying the whole of the organization. Managers who oversee day-to-day work can be enormously agentic in helping their team members access meaning.

Pattakos and Dundon say that the fundamental role of leadership is to help people find and connect to the deeper meaning of their own work and then create the conditions within the culture that enable others to search for and discover meaning in their work. The low engagement in organizations occurs in part because the way it has been stewarded does not consider that everyone in the organization is responsible for creating a culture of meaning. Low engagement scores in organizations are indicative of employees' lack of trust in each other, that their work really matters, or has a deeper meaning, contributing to a greater good.[33]

When leaders create a culture and communicate how each person's role contributes to the purpose or mission of the organization, vitalizing meaning is activated.

Taking the human ability for self-transcendence into account, "good work" is then equal to "meaningful work," and "meaningful work," in turn, refers to work that brings something that exists into something better. In short, it brings something good closer to perfection.[34]

As the notion of responsibility is a central aim in logotherapy – to encourage people to take responsibility for their own lives, understanding the role of motivation and how it can be increased for efficacy and productivity is paramount. The logotherapeutic approach seeks to enable people to tap into their own motivational resources by pulling them toward what they most care about and value in life and setting themselves in motion toward attaining or experiencing it.

Key Points Summary

❖ The workforce hungers for meaning – give it to them, and you win and elevate the consciousness of your full ecosystem of stakeholders.

❖ Logotherapy is a fancy term that offers a simple way to activate the intrinsic motivation of your people in a way that treats their life malaise and elevates their well-being.

❖ Recognize that your organization offers one of the best playgrounds for people through work to realize their highest potential – don't squander that dynamic energy.

❖ It's critical to cascade the capacity to manage through meaning to your managers who touch the lives of your people every day.

5

O: Ownership Culture that Unites All Stakeholders Through Purpose (Who)

For business to reach its fullest potential in the twenty-first century, we need a new paradigm that moves beyond simplistic machine/industrial models to one that embraces the complexity and interdependencies in which corporations exist today. A new, evolutionary way to embrace this complexity and recognize interdependence is to embrace the paradigm of seeing your business as a Living Organization, as discussed in Chapter 2. Relating to your business as such enables an interactive relationship with all your stakeholders (customers, employees, investors, suppliers, and the community).[1] The optimal way to nurture and fortify those essential parties is to fully enroll and unite them around your organization's purpose. Doing so generates an incredibly dynamic force of combined synergies that operate as attentive, engaged owners (as opposed to temporary renters) while enjoying the regenerative fulfillment and "lift" from the association.

You have something very special to offer this ecosystem of stakeholders you depend on – a chance to know their lives matter. How you relate to each of them and communicate the promise of your organizational purpose and their contribution to realizing it is the differentiator. People ache to live meaningful lives. Give them that precious gift, and you amplify your own capacity to matter as an organization, which, done well, often translates to higher profit. In the words of Rabbi Daniel Cohen:

> Throughout the history of humanity, humans have striven to become immortal. From Ponce de Leon's quest for the fountain of youth to the building of monuments, we strive to outlast our mortality and defeat death. This isn't because we know we can physically transcend the limits of time but because programmed into our DNA is a desire to be remembered, to lead a life of significance. We all want to know we have made some everlasting contribution to the world.[2]

By giving your stakeholders the opportunity to contribute to something larger than themselves, and aligning themselves with your organizational purpose, you are positioned to vitalize this essential group of "who" beyond measure. This chapter distinguishes purpose and how operating from it matters in today's evolved conscious world. You'll learn what is required for companies to operate in what has been termed "the purpose economy" and you'll be introduced to a way to dynamically embed purpose into your stakeholder community by creating your own "parliament of purpose."

What is Purpose, and Why Does it Matter?

Purpose is hard to argue with, but what exactly is it? A term that has become ubiquitous in parlance, it has been woefully underutilized as a life or business imperative. On an individual level, I like Zach Mercurio's[3] definition of purpose as your rare and unique reason for existence that betters the world. Alicia Hare defines purpose as "the quiet, ever-present call inside each of us, that when followed, guides us to become the fullness of our potential" and is "the ultimate act of showing up."[4] Organizationally, we can think of purpose as the reason your company exists *and* why anyone should care.

Purpose works its wonders largely because our lives are finite, which gives an urgency to live them deeply and fully each day. But it takes real effort – what I refer to as "wild, alive scratching" to discover, stay tuned into, and live fully and productively that purpose. The world – and companies who wish to work from such advantage – need a rapid awakening of every member to discover their purpose, to determine what brings them most alive and illuminate who they've always been – and are becoming. We need fewer people just looking for and talking about purpose and more of them actively in service of it.[5] A critical component to vital well-being is that each person and entity can own their own purpose and articulate it powerfully as part of their identity.[6]

Purpose offers a critical directional compass in life that helps people orient life and work decisions and be energized to contribute their gifts through the lens of it.[7] Living and serving from purpose is incredibly vitalizing.[8] It has a built-in expansive element to it in that, when people work from purpose, they naturally serve others beyond themselves (which makes the world better), constantly grow their own capacity and persons/entities in service of this purpose because it evolves in our service to it, and allows people to cultivate and grow a community of nurturing relationships around them.[9] In other words, purpose provides a foundation for ongoing positive reverberation through all stakeholders.

Purpose does not function as an "on or off" switch, but rather a journey – a trek – an expedition that never ends. Purpose has been identified by Peele[10] through the progression of four stages across life, while Woods[11] illustrates it in 12 in accordance with the level of human consciousness achieved. Any way you look at it, purpose is a deep well from which to draw intense fulfillment, energy, and unique contribution. Living one's purpose, as a leader or company, magnetizes people of similar values toward you. The more we lean into purpose and live and work from it, the bigger our expression of usefulness. This usefulness, expressed as our purpose, is vast, complex, and ever unfolding, an idea I showcase in an anthology of 25 women from across the globe who have discovered and are serving from their purpose today.[12]

Many leaders mistakenly think of purpose functionally or instrumentally, regarding it as a tool they can wield. Contrast that with what Gulati refers to as "deep purpose" leaders who

[T]hink of it as something more fundamental: an existential statement that expresses the firm's very reason for being. Rather than simply pursuing a purpose, these leaders project it faithfully out onto the world. In their hands, purpose serves as an organizing principle that shapes decision-making and binds stakeholders to one another.[13]

Purpose is never about a focus on revenue and profit – it's about solving the problems and challenges of the people you wish to serve.[14] In other words, purpose has a self-transcendent quality about it and is *always* anchored in serving others. I was speaking at a business conference in September 2021 and heard a fellow speaker belt out with the boldest of confidence, "My purpose is to *double my income!*" I was immediately nauseous and frightened for her audience who she had just woefully misinformed. Her declaration was a personal *goal*, not her purpose. Revenue and profit are magnificent and even, I would say, *sexy*, but do not conflate purpose with profit. They are wholly distinct ideas, which can be distinguished as a relationship between the extent to which an entity (person or business) serves its why resulting in the size of its profit.

The same misguided declarations occur in companies in the form of "purpose washing," akin to "green washing" which speaks to dim-veiled attempts at ecologically friendly activities in hopes of fostering favor among communities. The term "purpose" has been deployed superficially by companies to appear virtuous without the benefit of using it as a core operational principle. Companies that treat purpose as an existential intention that informs every decision, practice, and process are thriving in today's times where business is expected to be a force for good in the world. This new breed of stakeholder capitalism adopts purpose as their operating system, perceiving it as a vital animating force with near-spiritual power. As a result, these companies can navigate the tumultuous terrain of multi-stakeholder capitalism far more adeptly than most, increasing value for all stakeholders, including investors, over the long term. Completely overused to the point of obsolescence, for example "pancakes, on purpose," "tires, on purpose," and the like are exactly the opposite of what's advocated in this chapter.

People "gain purpose when they grow personally, when they establish meaningful relationships, and when they are in service to something greater than themselves."[15] "We find purpose when we do things we love, attempt new challenges, and express our voice to the world."[16] Purpose is not a cause, revelation, or luxury – but rather a choice and a journey.[17]

Company purpose answers the question, "why does the organization exist, and why should anyone care?" Soulful purpose is the core reason a company exists, and the mission is how it is expressed through its products and services. The vision is the articulation of what the world will look like in the future when the soulful purpose is more fully realized.[18] Purpose as a statement should be incredibly inspiring to everyone in the organization. The most compelling purpose statements contain two basic and interrelated features: they "delineate an ambitious, longer-term goal for the company," and "they give this goal an idealistic cast, committing the firm to fulfillment of broader social duties."[19] On top of all this, purpose is not only good for business but a driving force within it.

Purpose as Today's Driving Business Imperative

Today's business requires strength in purpose and execution. Organizations with a strong sense of purpose but lacking capacity to execute it will ultimately die, while organizations that are expert executors but fail to understand and see the value of purpose cannot reach their full potential.[20] It may surprise you to learn that, seemingly overnight, we have crept into living in the "purpose economy," where people expect meaning and purpose in life and work. I learned this perspective by reading Aaron Hurst's book, *The Purpose Economy*,[21] which was so delightfully alluring, I had to invite him as a guest on *Working on Purpose*[22] to delve further into his ideas. He describes the Purpose Economy as "the new context and set of ways in which people and organizations are focused on creating value, and it defines the organizing principle for innovation and growth."[23]

It's useful and rather arresting to recognize how much economic life has advanced in just the last two decades. Consider the four distinct economies Hurst identifies in recent US history: agrarian (to 1750), industrial (to 1950), information (to 2000+), and purpose (present, since 2008). He says that, in large part, the purpose economy was ushered in by both an increasing number of Millennials in the workplace who valued meaning and purpose across their lives, and the instability of the marketplace after the 2008 recession, which encouraged people to look for stability in themselves, not employers, and placed meaning and purpose at the heart of the desired work experience.[24]

These four economies, it seems to me, indicate the unfoldment and elevation of human consciousness. How are consciousness and purpose related? Organizations that embrace the path to meaning and purpose for all stakeholders inherently make the world a better place. They are then positioned to listen to the call of what humanity, our ecology, the unborn, and the cosmos are asking us to do to survive, thrive, evolve, an idea we touched on in Chapter 2, and brought to us by Peele. Hoyos stated in her book, *Purpose: The Ultimate Quest*, that only 1% of the global population is fully living their purpose. When that number gets to 3%, she says, human consciousness will be raised such that peace is actually possible.[25] I think that's worth getting up for. Working toward that possibility compels my work with leaders to create cultures anchored in meaning in companies led by purpose while making work the playground that best enables individuals to realize their potential.

What this means for your organization is that your people will be motivated and perform at their best when they personally know the purpose of your organization and how their contribution aligns with and supports that purpose. By now you know that purpose has become unignorable in today's business world. Customers insist you serve from it, and team members will only stay with you and contribute their best if you live by it. Many leaders don't understand that the pursuit of purpose as an organization enhances business performance. When pursued "deeply," it galvanizes organizations and generates outsized performance which helps focus strategy-making, fosters relationships with customers, deepens engagement with external stakeholders, and inspires employees.[26] It takes keeping your organization's purpose present and fully living it for your team members to feel the necessary sense of ownership to it. You will learn more about how you can steward consciousness in yourself and your organization in Chapter 8, Wake the Soul.

Operating from purpose has many advantages, as Tim Jones, aka "The Grow Good Guy" and New Zealand's #1 B Corp and Purpose Specialist, and I discussed on *Working on Purpose*.[27] Jones touts such advantages of operating from purpose as enjoying higher purpose-driven performance among the team, boosted employee happiness and engagement, and being able to attract the best talent who demand meaning and purpose. He also lists being able to net more and committed customers who are drawn to your company purpose, being able to elicit investment for growth, and being able to create a real legacy through your leadership from purpose. As if these benefits were not already sufficiently enticing, Jones says that purpose is contagious and is "the self-saucing chocolate cake of goodness." Howard Shore brings the power of purpose-inspired service home in his book, *The Leader Launchpad: Five Steps to Fuel Your Business and Lift Your Profits*,[28] when he says:

> You know you have a strong understanding of the customer when you have the lowest cost of customer acquisition in your industry, your growth rates are astronomical and your sales people become order takers and you, and your biggest challenge is scaling fast enough.[29]

Once you realize how purpose can distinguish your brand, mobilize and unite all your stakeholders, *and* infuse *you* with vital energy and focus, why would you want to return to a lower level of conscious business? You will learn more about how you can steward consciousness in yourself and your organization in Chapter 8, Wake the Soul.

Your Parliament of Purpose

The opportunity beckons, and the imperative commands to reach deeply, creatively, and constantly to *all* your stakeholders and live your company's purpose deeply while encouraging and enabling them individually to connect and be enlarged by it. Doing so unleashes a veritable cascade of support that will raise your business to completely new heights of flourishing. Purpose provides a framework for building an ecosystem of long-term partnerships with all stakeholders. Purpose facilitates collaboration by defining shared "superordinate" goals, which are larger goals that require collaboration to realize, that partners can agree on, and behind which they can rally.[30]

> When we fuse forces in teams, cultures, and societies that are tapping into the higher angels of our nature, we can create exponential outcomes that even the best, brightest, and most powerful individuals cannot do on their own. This is what Brene Brown refers to as *collective effervescence*.[31]

To reinforce a longer-term focus, as advocated in Chapter 1, Gumption, Milano advocates that you create an ownership culture which all managers participate in, and assume responsibility for decisions, results, and consequences, as discussed in this chapter. When each manager and each employee accept their business obligations as if they owned them, organizations create more value.[32] Further, Milano expounds:

> To reinforce the business management processes and all the training and communication, properly designed compensation can provide owner-like upside opportunity as well as downside accountability. Why make managers choose between what's good for the company and what's good for themselves and their family? Companies that embrace an ownership culture develop better strategies, improve execution, and deliver more profit and cash flow. And this all culminates in higher total shareholder return, greater compensation, and more secure jobs. Like most things worth doing, embracing an ownership culture requires considerable effort. Yet it provides defensible competitive advantages that are difficult to replicate.[33]

When the goal the organization is working towards connects with the individual purpose of team members, they become naturally committed to the larger entity. It's a symbiotic relationship: as they deliver their own personal purpose, they simultaneously deliver and amplify the organization's purpose.[34]

Let's look at a new way for you to think about the matter of purpose and how to create a culture of ownership around it. First, I'll provide the context of how this approach evolved and came to be. It started with my friend and colleague Diane McClay, a Personal Empowerment and Career Transformation Coach,[35] and her knowledge of my love of owls. Not only are they considered symbols of wealth, fortune, wisdom, prosperity, and good luck, but I also regard them as elegant, confident, and alluring. As we were preparing for a purpose retreat we were co-facilitating, she began to ponder what a group of owls is called, and discovered a vast repertoire of language to describe groups of birds in her search. For example, we use such language as a flock of doves, a gaggle of geese, and a murder of crows. An exultation of larks, a bouquet of pheasants, and a bevy of quail. What's a group of owls called? A *parliament. A parliament of owls.* Why not, then, assemble a Parliament of Purpose for your organization – a collection of like-minded, heart-aligned stakeholders in a nurturing and supportive eco-system of interdependence? This human-centric perspective sees customers, employees, suppliers, and communities not as entities to produce and serve *for* but rather to produce and serve *with.* This stance goes beyond maximizing shareholder profit and reaches toward optimizing stakeholders both inside and outside your organization, instead of allowing the process or structure to dictate decision-making and direction.[36] Uniting all your stakeholders together and enrolling them in your organization's purpose, galvanizes the company and can generate greater performance.[37]

As you consider the interests of each of your stakeholder communities, it's critical that you keep your actions and words focused on embedding deep purpose into every atom of your organization, as Gulati counsels. Doing so handily rewards you with four distinct benefits. The first is the directional benefit that serves as your organization's "North Star" to guide your strategy, decision-making, and innovation. The relational benefit helps you sustain credibility and trust with ecosystem partners and establish long-term relationships. Deep purpose helps you build affinity, loyalty, and trust with customers, illustrating the reputational benefit. Fourth, the motivational benefit of running your business from deep purpose yields an inspired and motivated workforce in a way few other tools can.[38] Consciously led organizations are increasingly creating stakeholder maps to orient their focus and visually display their dynamic interdependencies to serve the whole ecosystem. We'll briefly treat each of the communities pertinent to most organizations, though you may have a distinctive addition or two.

Employees: By now, you know a strong and undeniable purpose should be core to your organization's DNA and "people working for your company and customers should know and understand how your organization contributes to the world and believe its existence is necessary."[39] Your team members should know your company's purpose statement and be able to recite it verbatim – not as a rote exercise but because they feel meaningfully connected to it. Then they can actively speak about, promote, and get others excited about helping to fulfill this purpose. That creates limbic resonance among the team and powerfully binds them in meaningful relationship toward realizing a mission much bigger than themselves. With your organization's purpose firmly understood in the minds and hearts of your team members, they become motivated catalysts to fulfill the purpose.[40] Advertising this employer brand attracts people aligned to the purpose and values of your organization and distinguishes your work opportunity from others.

One way to make your purpose really *live* inside your organization is to routinely bring in customers who have benefitted from the products or services you provide, a practice Michigan-based medical equipment manufacturing company Stryker has been doing quite effectively for years. Louis Efron, guest on *Working on Purpose*, author of *Purpose Meets Execution*, and previous team member of Stryker, talked about how his former employer helps keep its purpose alive by showing employees at all levels how their work helps the company live its mission to make healthcare better.[41] Stryker does so by bringing in people whose lives have been improved or saved through the medical devices they make. Through these shares, employees feel enlarged, their own purpose extended, as members of Stryker.

Shore further situates the benefits of purpose. "Having your employees act with purpose will inspire change. When you act with purpose, you respond with more energy and enthusiasm. When your company purpose is important to people, they volunteer for extra work and take on challenges and problems."[42] As the workforce majority continues to arc toward the younger generations of the Millennials and Gen Z, meaning and purpose are center-stage requirements in the workplace. As Dr. Holly Woods and I discussed on *Working on Purpose*,[43] as younger generations are now able to take advantage of 60 expansive years of human and spiritual development, and make use of traditional and alternative modalities for healing, the youngest boomers, Gen X, Millennials (Gen Y), and Gen Z cohorts have begun to more rapidly move into higher levels of consciousness and purpose expression than their more seasoned counterparts in the older Boomer and Traditionalist generations. This means the younger generations in the workforce have not only been groomed through their upbringing and culture to earlier discover their own purpose and access their meaning systems, but they will also not tolerate work and life that does not align with such imperatives.

Customers: Customers are increasingly voting econom- ically, seeking to do business with companies sharing their values. When your organizational purpose aligns with their perspective on an ideal world, and their values, you are much more likely to retain and deepen those customer relationships. Just because purpose boosts reputation doesn't mean it attracts all customers. Living your purpose means you will also be less appealing to some customers who don't share your company's values or who have concerns that they regard as competing, in which case they are better served elsewhere. People living in the purpose economy put less emphasis on cost, convenience, and function of products and services, and more on decisions to increase meaning in their lives, buying products and services that fulfill that need. A strong case can be argued for this imperative undergirding the success of the high-end grocery store Whole Foods. Sometimes nicknamed "Whole Paycheck" in reference to its higher prices compared to other options, Whole Foods appeals to a loyal customer base for its fresh and healthy food selections, fair trade practices, and attentiveness to employees with higher-than-industry-standard pay and benefits even for part-time workers.

Suppliers: Suppliers are essential to the success of your business, and how you treat them dictates their dedication and support to your business. Choosing suppliers that align with your purpose and values in how you like to do business greatly increases their dedication to performing their best for you. Those suppliers will go the extra mile when they feel they are part of your organization, realizing its purpose, which then enlivens and enlarges their own impact. Consciously led companies are increasingly trying to select suppliers they intend to positively benefit, and help to lift their financial prosperity, whether they are minority-owned businesses or others whose operations align with or extend a value held by the buying company. For example, you may opt to do business with a company run or powered by veterans or people who have spent time in prison to leverage your business to better the world, akin to the "beautiful business" model discussed in Chapter 1, Gumption, in a mutual exchange that allows you to simultaneously enrich their dedication and commitment to you.

Community/Society: Community awareness of who your company is and how you are behaving allows you to mobilize brand communities and build movements of people, comprised of both current customers and those for whom you aspire.[44] As discussed in Chapter 3, Sustainability, the community and your full complement of stakeholders increasingly care about your perspective and actions taken on environmental, social, and governance (ESG) matters. For example, Charles Antis, CEO and Owner of Antis Roofing and Waterproofing in California, leveraged their people and resources during the pandemic to bring food to first responders and seniors and to organize blood drives, which was part of their efforts to show solidarity.[45] How do you want to relate to your community? Knowing what you want to stand for and how you can be relied upon is part of building a solid ecosystem.

Investors: How about your current or potential investors? Do they care about purpose, and specifically, yours? You bet they do. Increasingly, there is a movement toward shareholders seeking purpose-led organizations in which to invest because these organizations increase long-term profitability, gain more customers, and better retain employees.[46] Communicating well and living your purpose authentically to distinguish your products and services captures the hearts and wallets of those who believe in your cause and want to help enable your fuller expression.

Planet: There is a sixth stakeholder also in existence today, and that's the planet. Being mindful and communicating how your company's operations impact the planet through energy use, waste and recycling, and other environmental impacts is no longer an action to take "when you get around to it." The reasons are covered in Chapter 3, Sustainability, and won't be rehashed here, but suffice it to say that the planet has finally earned its rightful place in the stakeholder community.

Though it may seem overwhelming at first to consider the needs and desires of all these stakeholder communities, thoughtfully planning to serve and lift them through your operations greatly enlivens the vitality of the ecosystem and enables you to better execute purpose and profits: how you generate your own dynamic Parliament of Purpose. Crafting it involves bringing key representatives from each stakeholder community together in a strategic purpose alignment session and nurtured over time, an activity further discussed in Chapter 8 – Wake.

Key Points Summary

- ❖ Your organization's purpose serves to inspire team members to give their best to fulfill it, while guiding all actions, decisions, and choices. Lived and fully activated, it serves as a beacon and unites your stakeholders powerfully together in service of it.
- ❖ Facilitate and steward an ownership culture throughout your organization where everyone has "skin in the game" to keeping it growing, thriving, and successful.
- ❖ Purpose is no longer a "nice to have" feature in business. Rather, the workforce expects it, customers opt in or out of you because of it, and investors seek purpose-led companies for the greater value they produce and return on investment they yield.
- ❖ By creating and nurturing your "parliament of purpose," comprised of your full stakeholder community, you powerfully connect all parties and create a force larger than the sum of its parts, all singing from the same sheet of music to work toward your company's purpose.

PART 2
The "How" Through NOW

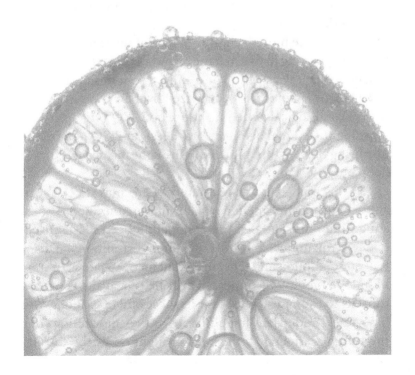

Having read the five chapters of Part 1, you have a lay of the land of the "What" to situate your business in the world you are operating in today. You better understand the forces that have driven the Great Resignation of people rapidly leaving their jobs without another yet secured and what the workforce now desires and expects. Their quest to work for an organization that stands to make a positive impact and aligns with their values compels them to move toward a company better suiting those values. People want improved work-life harmony than they enjoyed prior to the forced lockdown of the COVID pandemic and seek work situations that allow it, whether through remote or hybrid work or flex schedules. A focus on sustainability means the workforce is watching and evaluating your company's words and deeds on the matter and will opt into or out of working with you accordingly. By now, you are more in tune with the depth of meaning and purpose today's workforce craves. Find more ways to give them access to it, and you win in the purpose economy we live in today.

In Part 2, we move from the "What" of the world you find yourself operating in to teach the "How" of instituting cultural practices that unleash gusto and enliven your business. These practices, by chapter, are categorized by their roots in IQ (or rational and logical structural processes), EQ (emotional or meaning-fueled management practices), and SQ (spiritually nurturing leadership practices through the execution of deep purpose).

By this point in your reading, you are now much more aware of the environment in which your organization is operating. Your mind and heart have hopefully been substantively opened. You understand you have an opportunity to dig deep for your gumption and let yourself fall in love again with your business by getting reconnected to its heartbeat and your own capacity to exercise agency over its successful operations. You have a new understanding of the urgency commanding your response occasioned by the swirl brought on by the COVID

pandemic, changes in values toward a greater work-life harmony, and an employee-led marketplace, all commingling to
incentivize your swift response. You've learned how crucial
your company operations and your actions as a leader must
be to operate sustainably and communicate to your stakeholders as such that you are. You now understand the "Therapy" that is readily available by activating meaning potentials
and logotherapy to energize and motivate your stakeholders
to execute your mission. Finally, you recognize the power of
a shared sense of ownership that uniting your stakeholders
offers around your company purpose.

What might the world, and your company or business,
look like when the GUSTO solutions explored in Part 1
are applied and lived? What if you could transform your
business into a teeming laboratory where your stakeholders
learn, grow, and thrive, while dynamically executing your
company purpose? Where you activate a vibrant ecosystem
of stakeholders impassioned to your company purpose and
committed to its execution? To help you navigate the new
landscape of today's times, you need to employ a holistic
leadership approach that reaches toward ongoing higher
consciousness, first in yourself, and then in and across your
whole organization. Part 2 provides a set of best practices to
activate meaning and purpose throughout your organization,
culture, and operations. In short, Part 2 shows you HOW you
can implement the GUSTO solutions NOW. Each chapter
is organized around one area of intelligence, advancing
sequentially along each of the three utilized, as follows.

Chapter 6 on Nurture Through Mindfulness is organized
from the premise of the long-standing area of rational intelligence – IQ, or intelligence quotient, which measures the ability to analyze, reason, think abstractly, use language, visualize,
and comprehend (and corresponds to the mind and left-brain
thinking).[1] The IQ measure has been used since the beginning
of the twentieth century[2] and here entails employing intellect
and cognition to review and replace any obsolete processes

and procedures that touch your people against the backdrop of today's standard as outlined in Part 1 (i.e., especially to address the desire for meaning and purpose). It advocates for understanding the unique needs and interests of each team member and overhauling archaic processes and procedures that hamper the human spirit at work.

With IQ holding strong as a basis for competence in leaders as well as individual contributors since the early 1900s, Chapter 7, Open the Heart, centers on practices anchored in emotional intelligence (EQ), which was introduced in 1990 and made popular by Daniel Goleman and his book, *Emotional Intelligence,* in 1995. Emotional intelligence is "a form of social intelligence that involves the ability to monitor one's own and others' feelings and emotions, to discriminate among them, and to use this information to guide one's thinking and action,"[3] and corresponds to right-brain thinking. Thus, the practices recommended in this chapter are designed to appeal to the emotional realm and open the hearts of all your stakeholders by activating meaning in everyday encounters of the business operations and inspiring impassioned action toward the realization of your organizational mission.

Chapter 8, Wake the Soul, then progresses to practices anchored in a new area of intelligence – SQ, or spiritual intelligence.

> Spiritual intelligence is a higher dimension of intelligence that activates the qualities and capabilities of the authentic self (or the soul), in the form of wisdom, compassion, integrity, joy, love, creativity, and peace. Spiritual intelligence results in a sense of deeper meaning and purpose, combined with improvements in a wide range of important life skills and work skills.[4]

SQ has nothing to do with religion and is not belief – or faith-based – it is the new secular scientific paradigm of spirituality.[5] Ayala Domani, citing Stephen R. Covey, says he defines Spiritual Quotient as conscience, "having the following characteristics: enthusiastic, intuitive, takes responsibility, moral, wise, integrity, servant, humble, fair, ethical, abundant, compassionate, respectful, and cause-oriented," and is the central and most fundamental of all the intelligences because it becomes the source of guidance for the other two[6] and can be considered as whole-brain thinking. This chapter focuses on how leaders can develop their individual consciousness to raise and steward such development among individual team members throughout and set the course for an ongoing, forward-reaching organization ever mindful of its ecosystemic operations.

N: Nurture Through Mindfulness (IQ)

So much of everyday life happens on autopilot. We rise from bed in the same posture, brush our teeth in the exact same way, and towel off from the shower in the same fashion we did the day prior. We drive to our home or office often without any recollection of the path we took to get there, so ingrained is the behavior. A full 95% of our behavior is unconsciously chosen. These automated habits make it possible for us to conserve our energies from those repetitious tasks and divert that precious mental capacity elsewhere.

While this autopilot approach to basic personal chores allows efficiencies, it's a killer for your living, breathing company, whose very existence and ongoing vitality are dependent on the team members who power it. To remain strong and vibrant in a constantly evolving world requires ongoing vigilance and conscious intervention for sustenance and growth. It is critical that you stay present to the heartbeat of your company and the health of all its stakeholders. Very likely, your organization has accumulated antiquated ways of operating that are literally killing the organism you depend on the most to operate your business – your team members. To create a workplace where they actually want to come to work and do their best, you need to harness your IQ skills and mindfully evaluate the extent to which your current people processes and procedures are working for or against you.

Fifty years ago, the life expectancy of a Fortune 500 company was about 75 years. Now it is less than 15.[1] This challenging, ever-changing environment demands constant scrutiny and the consideration of new ways of thinking about business operations. High-performing companies recognize theirs are living organizations that are at their strongest when they focus on their ongoing evolution, ever stewarding their culture and with continuous focus on serving all stakeholders in their ecosystem, all whilst considering the impact of operations on the environment. These companies steward consciousness among their employees[2] by providing ongoing learning and development. This chapter highlights some key areas recommended for examination and likely overhaul to create a destination workplace your people will be reticent to leave. Starting with conducting a human capital audit on all your processes and procedures to discern improvements that elicit more enriching connection and personal expression in the workplace, to instituting a culture of focusing on strengths rather than weaknesses and areas to be "fixed," and retiring any "high performance" employee development focus. You will learn how performing ongoing employee engagement research to measure and improve it not only elevates understanding of areas to improve but also increases connection by opening dialogue between management and team members. Finally, you will learn how opening your receptivity to the changing geographic demands on your workforce increases their affinity for you as an employer of choice and how thoughtfully incorporating artificial intelligence and robotics measures to relieve monotony and increase productivity elevates fulfillment.

Perform a Human Capital Process and Procedure Audit

You learned in Chapters 2, Urgency, and 4, Therapy, about the dismally low engagement rate among the general workforce as reported by the Gallup Organization – with only 20% of the global workforce engaged in the work they do.[3] That figure is at least partly so because the leaders inside many organizations do not see people as individuals, wholly unique beings with special talents – but rather as "human resources" to be dispatched or engaged in a set of tasks. The archaic practices have taken hold because they satisfy the organization's need for control. Large organizations are complex places, and a strong and understandable instinct of their leaders is to seek simplicity and order – at least in part because this makes it easier to persuade themselves and their stakeholders that they are moving toward their objectives.[4] The problem with relying on old command and control procedures is they suck the life out of the very people you depend on to fuel the performance of your company. Instead, looking through a human-centric lens, and to activate meaning and purpose in your workplace, conduct a human capital process and procedure audit. Finding such "obsoledge," Westphal's freshly minted term to describe outdated information, and updating procedures with front-line employee input can radically improve productivity and morale simultaneously.

When performing a human capital audit, consider the full life cycle of your employees – from attraction to you through your employment brand and promise on your careers website, to your recruitment and interview process, to onboarding new team members and training them, to your organizational structure, performance evaluation, promotion, separation, and more. I can virtually guarantee your organization is utilizing not just outdated processes but ones that alienate and diminish the very hearts and souls you count on to fulfill your mission. Your goal is to become a human-centric enterprise that optimizes the employee experience instead of allowing the process or structure to dictate decision-making and direction at their expense.[5]

Another important area to evaluate is work task flow. Rather than blame poor performance on non-motivated employees, you are far better served to go looking for what they are up against to do their job well. In your investigation, you may be surprised to learn the work-arounds employees create just to make things work or to serve a customer.[6] Auditing task flow must entail learning directly from those on the front line performing the work, and then solutioning through a combination of their input and a fresh outside search for best practices.

When it comes to giving team members more autonomy and unleashing creativity and responsibleness, consider structuring teams through "holacracy." Through a social technology for governing and operating a team, holacracy takes the best from "Getting Things Done" and "Agile" approaches to yield a dynamic approach to collaboration and productivity. It involves continually evolving the team structure based on small experiments and new information. Everything starts in holacracy with "tension"; consider where things are not going the way you want. With holacracy, you can use this tension as fuel for moving forward and improving productivity while developing the skills of each team member.[7]

Another critical area to evaluate in your company is compensation. Upon examination, many leaders come to realize they are incentivizing behavior that does not align with their stated objectives. Consider the trouble Wells Fargo got into in 2016 as employees felt pressure to make sales quotas and resorted to an array of fraudulent activities, including opening fake accounts and extending credit lines, all without the consent of their customers. As you review your compensation policies, consider Milano's ideas to incentivize all employees to perform as if "owners," as introduced in Chapter 5. Briefly, he advocates for using residual cash earnings to measure performance, as doing so spreads the benefits of investments over time, which in turn encourages greater investment in the future while holding managers accountable for returns on investments.[8]

A few other immediate areas to review, especially in times of high turnover such as we're experiencing during the Great Resignation, are dress codes, static work schedules, forced ranking, and no telecommuting (discussed more in detail later in this chapter). Relaxing policies on when your employees can start or end their workday to accommodate their personal needs to care for loved ones or exercise indicates you value their well-being and can provide an immediate halt to those quickly making their way to the exit. Scrutinize anything that smacks of "that's the way we've always done it," including your policy on length of time an employee must remain in a job before applying for and being considered for another. Many companies require one or two years in a job before being "permitted" to apply for another within the company. Many people value learning, growth, and development, and being strapped in a chair extinguishes their achievement motive and sends them looking for opportunity elsewhere.

Focus On and Nurture Individual Strengths

Over the years of practicing as a management consultant, I've considered deeply just what "growth" means for people. The answer I have come to is this: an ever-building awareness of competency, contribution, fulfillment, and impact. What would happen in your company if instead of noticing and looking for what's *wrong* with team members and their performance, you instead went forth with ferocious curiosity to study and celebrate what makes them delightfully *different* and distinguishes the way they do things? As a long-time Gallup-certified Strengths Coach, I have facilitated hundreds of sessions for corporations, small companies, non-profits, schools, and families to discover that which makes each person in attendance unique and special. I continue to be amazed at the frequency with which I encounter people well into their careers who have never discovered their strengths. In their newfound understanding of how their top five (of 34 talent themes) inform their preferences for behaving and communicating, they both understand how they're best motivated at work and where conflict arises with other team members who approach work from their own strengths set.

Organizations that make it a practice to help their workforce discover their strengths and unique talents, and then encourage and reward their use, are the winners in today's meaning-insistent times. To clarify, a strength is not something you're good at (that's an ability or skill); a strength is "an activity that makes you *feel* strong."[9] Working from strengths gives people three distinct powerful, intrinsically motivating feelings: anticipation beforehand, flow during, and fulfillment after. Working from strengths speaks more to appetite than ability, so your best opportunity as a leader is to help each individual team member discover his or her strengths and then encourage and enable their use in their daily work.

Completely railing against the adage that the best people are well rounded, how delightful to learn that, no, "[q]uite the opposite, in fact – *the best people are spiky,* and in their lovingly honed spikiness they find their biggest contribution, their fastest growth, and ultimately, their greatest joy."[10] Enliven your workplace by instilling in your culture the practice of noticing and rewarding the distinctive way your team members perform their work, their own "spikiness," which helps them understand and revel in their own uniqueness and further motivates them to continue contributing their talents. Conduct strengths discovery sessions with a certified Gallup Strengths Coach to help your team distinguish their own unique contributions, and then encourage each team member to bring their best "spike" to complement the dynamic of the team. A common mistake I see leaders and managers make is that they seek and reward people who approach performance and communication in a manner similar to their own. The result is a shocking lack of diversity in talent and a dismal display of innovation. Be the leader who goes looking for and celebrates the spiky.

Banish Your "High Performance" Programs and Embrace "Momentum"

Neither companies, nor their people, are best served when they separate into "hi-po" and "low-po" groups, that is high potential or low potential. The process of separating into these groups is often done carelessly and with bias toward employees whose values, talents, and ethnicity often resemble that of the appointers, which then codifies and amplifies this bias. When a leader rates a team member as displaying high potential, the designee receives more training dollars and attention. A "high po" label will travel with them for a while and bestows a privilege denied to the rest of the employee population. The same is true if you give someone a low potential rating, which also travels with them and brands them as "less than" the other group. By designating a small group of people in your organization as "hi po," you have just unknowingly demotivated the vast majority of your workforce for whom you did not award the label.

To perform in today's dynamic marketplace, you need *all* your team members to be maximized, fully contributing their talents to your organization. A way forward is to embrace Marcus Buckingham and Ashley Goodall's approach to developing individual careers of your people by asking them two sets of questions: one is about who they are as a person and what they love (their traits and *mass*, as the authors describe it), and the other is how they've moved through the world so far which includes their past experience, performance, and what they've learned which can be measured (their states and *velocity*, as the authors call it). Taken together, and borrowing from physics, the authors combine mass and velocity to arrive at a concept called "*momentum.*" It's not a matter of whether any of your team members can learn and grow, but rather, *how*, how efficiently, and in what direction. Everyone has "potential," and it's just a matter of how to tap into it. Each person has a different momentum, and your opportunity as a leader is to swiftly move away from the "high-potential" limiting and exclusionary practice to enable the momentum in *everyone*.

Bob Chapman, long-time CEO of Barry-Wehmiller Companies, discovered for himself some years ago the magic of seeing all 12,000 of his "heart count" (as he likes to call each team member, as opposed to "head count") as "someone's precious child."[11] Bob's "aha" happened while attending a wedding and realizing during the ceremony that each of these people about to be married is someone's precious child, whose parents want them to be loved and cared for. That insight, combined with another at church listening to the sermon, combined to help Bob realize the pastor at his church has his congregants for one hour per week, while Barry-Wehmiller has all 12,000 of them for 40 hours per week! Bob realized that business has a great opportunity to lift and inspire all people in an organization – and celebrate that "everybody matters."[12] Bob's view on staffing a company is that it's not about getting the best people as it is enabling each person in the organization to be the best they can be.

When you move away from the de-humanizing approach of segmenting your team members into "high potential" or "not," you immediately unleash potential and momentum in them all. That is a much better return on investment than merely developing a small sub-set of the overall team. Instead, teach your managers to learn about human growth and motivating through strengths and prompt them to have conversations with their team members about their careers through the lens of "momentum," which naturally focuses on who the person is and where and how fast he or she is going in the world. Your people will be far less likely to respond to a call from a recruiter elsewhere when they feel seen, understood, and appreciated by you and their fellow team members. Invest in knowing their strengths and helping to develop them.

Re-Tool Feedback and Recognition

It is astounding how far a well-considered "thank you" can go, and yet many leaders have never bothered developing the skill or have gotten so busy handling the business or their department that it's been neglected. By feedback and recognition, I most certainly don't mean through the annual performance review process, which is an activity I recommend you entirely eradicate, if not greatly alter and develop. Roger Steinkruger, a 50-year healthcare veteran, the last 25 years of which were spent as a CEO, agrees: "In my years of experience, I have never seen anything good result from these types of systems. For the inspiring, loving, servant leader, adherence to such systems is discouraging, destructive, and disrespectful."[13] Simply giving your team members attention that you see them, notice their efforts, and give them feedback on what they do best and what they can improve goes a long way.[14] How to do so in an ongoing, sustainable way? Well, that takes folding it into your culture operations and management protocols. You can help your team members feel they are significant and that they matter simply by expressing consistent, meaningful, and personalized feedback and gratitude.[15]

A way to fold feedback and recognition into your culture is to train your management team to be on alert for team members who live your company purpose, go the extra mile to deliver on your mission, and exemplify your values. Depending on their preference for public or private recognition (and this is key – do not use a "one size fits all" approach with your team), you can celebrate the aligned behavior in one-on-one conversations, in team meetings, or the company newsletter spotlighting the team member. Rewarding team members who live your company purpose, mission, and values is an excellent way to keep them feeling meaningfully connected to your organization while modeling and teaching the behavior to other team members, especially the newer ones who don't have as much history of exposure to your culture.

The larger your company becomes, the more you'll likely need to incorporate a technology platform to help you scale recognition and feedback while also spreading the good sentiments among all team members. Doing so can create a powerful culture of recognition while also easing the heavy lifting from the manager who directly supervises the team member. I have learned about how to scale feedback and appreciation from Michael Levy, the CEO of Work Proud.[16] He and his company have essentially created a "Facebook page" for a company where all team members can weigh in and give a shout out and thanks to fellow members, creating a crescendo of positive engagement, thanks to the benefit of technology. The larger your organization becomes, the more you may benefit from ways to involve other team members and technology to build a culture of recognition across the company.

Meanwhile, I encourage you to learn to give thanks and appreciation in a way that is so meaningful to your team member that you move them to tears. Not because they are hurt or embarrassed, but because you have literally touched the very core of what matters to them and "seen" them for the unique, wonderful creatures they are and the contribution they have made. As author and poet Maya Angelou famously quipped, "People will forget what you said, people will forget what you did, but people will never forget how you made them feel."[17] To activate meaning, learn to say "thank you" and "you matter here" in a way people won't forget. While you're at it, bring that practice home and learn to tell your loved ones how they matter to you. Doing so will radically alter your organization and your personal relationships.

Measure and Increase Employee Engagement and Fulfillment

Today's workplace is constantly changing, and so are the desires of the workforce powering it. It is critical you stay on top of monitoring the engagement of your employees and learn where things are going well in their experience of working for you, and where things need shoring up. Conduct an anonymous annual employee engagement survey, ideally through a third party to ensure a separation of the gathering of the data and its reporting from anyone inside. Doing so also adds credibility of anonymity among the employees, so they can be candid and thus more helpful in their responses. You need to understand what's happening in your organization, and when communicated and executed well, an engagement survey provides actionable feedback to help your team make continual course corrections. It's critical to ask clear, actionable questions and creating them well should be informed by professionals skilled in research and analysis.

Be a leader worth following (see Chapter 8): when you get the results, good or bad, share them with the full organization, so they see and believe you received the feedback, listened to it, and understand their experience. Reporting the results also creates an accountability in you and your management team to do something about the results and communicate progress along the way so your people feel they are part of a learning, growing organization – just how you expect them to be. In other words, model the behavior you seek. When segregated by departments, you can learn where to apply more training to elevate the skills of managers and provide key resources for those teams to be more effective. Relate to the survey and its results as a dialogue and communication aid.

Next, help your employees understand that their own experience and relationship with their work is an essential aspect of their development and fulfillment. You can discern this in simple one-on-one conversations with their direct supervisor or manager. You can also use the Mode of Engagement discovery tool I developed some years ago. Over the course of a decade I investigated the manner in which people experience meaning in work and how it relates to their identity. I found 15 Modes of Engagement that illustrate a large spectrum of experience from extremely fulfilled and identified with one's work all the way to modes that diminish the person's self-esteem through work and hurl them into existential crisis (see Table 1 on pp. 142–3). A mode of engagement indicates a moment in time snapshot of how a person experiences their work in relation to their identity, captures the dynamic person-content exchange, and is mutable. Once people understand their experience of work, and gain clarity on what contributes to it being meaningful and motivating or not, the situation, context or way the work is performed can be addressed and improved.[18]

Deconstruct Time and Place in Today's Nimble Workplace

The genie is out of the bottle, and we can't put it back. By that I mean that people have discovered their lives work better with the flexibility working from home can provide. Giving up the autonomy that came with this discovery will be very difficult to pry from the workforce fingers. When so many people were forced to shelter-in-place, finding ways to be productive working from home, it changed, probably forever, our ideas about when and where work gets done. As Ranjay Gulati said in our on-air conversation, the COVID pandemic awakened people to want more from their lives.[19] You will win as a company when you find creative ways to mindfully question your current policies and practices of where work gets done in your business.

It can make sound business sense for companies to take a decentralized approach to organizational structures. Perform an analysis of the cost to maintain office or workspace for all employees – what if you could reduce the size of your structure to half and rotate your team on site instead of them working there daily? Consider how you could serve more customers if you could increase the standard work hours of the traditional 8 am to 5 pm and perhaps run from 6 am to 10 pm. Finally, the health and safety of your team can be improved through a virtual team setting by giving the ability to focus on tasks without interruption, reducing commute time to work sites, and increasing family connection. Consider how removing time and space can augment your operations to serve more customers and satisfy team members.

As mobility and geographic choice become increasingly important to people to manage their careers, consider new ways your company can offer choice or flexibility of location to entice and retain more desired talent. For example, Airbnb is giving their employees the opportunity to work remotely while greatly expanding upon this benefit by offering them the opportunity to work away from their country of residence, in any country of the world, for up to three months per year. Specifically, the company stipulates employees can choose to work from home or the office, and have the flexibility to travel and work around the world from any one of 180 countries for up to 90 days.[20] This geographic flexibility is a tremendous benefit and attractant, elevating Airbnb's desirable status among talent, and a delightful way to live its own purpose to "help create a world where you can belong anywhere and where people can live in a place, instead of just traveling to it."

As you consider deconstructing time and place in your organization, first identify the challenges you face in serving your customers and engaging the talents of your team members. Do your customers want to be able to contact you during what would otherwise be "off hours"? This may be an invitation to add coverage and people beyond your current confines of service. Next, what do your team members ideally want in their work arrangement to optimize their contribution and overall lives? Very likely, if your organization has been run from set schedules for everyone (i.e. 8 am to 5 pm), adding in some flex start/end hours can go a long way to accommodate the need to avoid congested travel commutes, allow dropping off kids at school in the morning, or handling other important non-work life events after work.

In today's fluid workplace, a best practice for many organizations is for team members to spend two days per week in the office or workplace (where possible, given the kind of work they do). Some companies are only requiring employees to come into the workplace one day per month, as "proof of life." When you do want or expect your team members to be in the office or workplace, it's important to tell them "why," what's in it for them, and how their togetherness benefits them and the effectiveness of the organization. As you consider the work arrangement opportunities, keep in mind ways you can create an environment that distinguishes and compels people to want to join and stay (i.e., do you encourage life-work harmony with this fluid schedule, do you operate from particular values that resonate with certain groups, etc.?).

Consider the options available to your organization.

a) Local: Your employees perform their work at the same location collectively each day, whether in the same building or in groups of buildings close enough to reach by walking or shuttle for meetings or collaboration.

b) Virtual: Your team members need to collaborate or communicate but are not in close proximity to walk or shuttle to meet.

c) Hybrid: Combination of local and virtual.[21]

No matter which of the options you choose to manage your teams, your managers and leaders need to continue developing their skills to be effective in motivating and guiding team members to their best performance and creating a place they want to remain. Virtual management requires a high level of commitment to personal communication with each team member. Virtual management requires less directive and more guiding and advising,[22] as well as outbound reach to keep the team connected.

You will need to invest in the development of your management and leadership team for them to be effective in a virtual or hybrid environment. Some personal qualities and characteristics to develop in your management to be successful in a virtual setting are: accessible, action-based, articulate, communicative, considerate, courageous, demonstrates integrity, expressive, fair-minded, honest, independent, intuitive, objective, passionate, proactive, self-motivated, straightforward, trustworthy.[23] Take honest stock in assessing your current team, then develop a plan and enroll the appropriate resources to bridge the gap in training, whether you enable in-house resources or secure third-party training to elevate the team's competence.

Finally, one last item to consider to effectively manage virtual or hybrid workforces is for each manager to create what Catherine Mattiske calls a "virtual team professional integrity code"[24] and I call a "team charter." It's best to do this when a virtual or hybrid team is formed but can be done at any time. The idea is to facilitate a team conversation about how work will get done, how the team is accountable to the standard, and the consequences of not living up to the code. This will make the job of the managers much more comfortable, especially if things go awry and team members do not perform to the standard agreed upon.

Elevate Your Team by Leveraging AI and Robotics

One of the underlying contributors to disengagement is the boredom that results from repetitive tasks. As people appreciate being challenged and learning new skills, look for opportunities in your organization to get your team focused on challenging, rather than mundane, repetitious work. Where can you find ways to re-imagine workflows and tasks to enable your team to use higher level skills and greater creativity, alongside technology? As you work to deploy artificial intelligence into your organization to elevate the work experience of your team, stay very focused on your core, humanistic purpose and communicate it clearly and often to every employee. For example, a consulting client I work with frequently sends similar emails to the same client over the course of a year. People in those jobs report boredom and a lack of stimulation and crave more meaningful work that challenges them to leverage their higher skills. A simple fix is to create an automated way to send those emails, freeing valuable creative and problem-solving skills to be leveraged for the client and elevating the engagement of the employee.

Many people fear technology, especially its role at work. Help your team understand how their jobs can become more interesting, and work toward alleviating their fear by helping them realize the elevating role technology can play in their lives and experience of work. The first step in your organization is to educate your team that your intent is to distinguish human and technological contribution in the workplace and improve the human experience at work: "[R]ather than using automation to replace human jobs, the goal of semi-automation is to build human-machine partnerships and elevate the work of humans."[25] When you help your team see the role of technology as a partnership, you help remove their fear and replace it with optimism and encouragement. Rather than considering artificial intelligence a threat to our unique humanity and our value within the workplace, we can instead think of it as a sophisticated partner, one that boosts our skills and ultimately elevates our contribution.

To thrive in the post-automation economy, it is necessary to develop in your team members "a twenty-first-century psyche" – that focuses on helping them "to be adaptable, mobile, constantly curious, optimistic and always learning, plus take charge of our destiny, be tenacious and have grit."[26] Just as the rise in automation to replace human jobs ushers in human-machine partnerships which require people undertaking continuous learning throughout their careers, your own leadership and business must continue to evolve and be performed at the highest standard.[27]

Artificial Intelligences learn from historical data and historical behaviors and thus reflect human bias and values. If your employees aren't fully aligned with your purpose, mission, vision and values, your AIs won't learn to be either.[28] It is critical for you as a leader to steward the technological transformation process and consciously protect the human experience you are trying to elevate. As such, any major automation effort should involve ethnographers and experienced designers on the front end of the project to understand the important steps where the innate humanity of the organization adds value within the business process. Poor awareness of where humans add unique value may lead to over-automated business processes that destroy market differentiation and reduce the company's ability to deliver against their brand promise and purpose.

The opportunity for people in the increasingly technology-abled world is to become more *human* – to double down on the skills technology simply cannot duplicate (which will be addressed in Chapter 7, Open the Heart). You can also use technology through virtual reality experiences to grow and meaningfully connect remote teams.[29] As you work to implement automation and AI to relieve mundane tasks and increase efficiencies, stay riveted on the human element in business.

> As technology becomes more capable, accurate, and fast at performing logical intelligence tasks such as machine learning and data analytics, human emotional intelligence and interpersonal and intrapersonal skills will become more important. These skills are required for organizations to understand human intentions, motivations, and desires and to act with diplomacy, courage, empathy, and enthusiasm for all stakeholders.[30]

In other words, embracing technology can allow people to experience more deeply their own humanity – to go beyond the intellectual, rational realm and more deeply develop emotional and relational capacities, an area that will be discussed next in Chapter 7.

Key Points Summary

❖ Perform a human capital process and procedure audit. The set of processes, procedures, and practice you use to run your organization greatly impact the productivity, vitality, and fulfillment of your employees and must be evaluated and updated to meet the standards of today's discerning workforce.

❖ Focus on and nurture individual strengths. It is incredibly debilitating for employees to be constantly scrutinized for what they are not doing well. Instead, focus on creating a culture where your managers look for what they do well and work to develop their strengths. Doing so also creates a greater capacity for them to hear and utilize constructive feedback to help them grow and improve.

❖ Banish your "high performance" programs. Abandon your "high potential" programs that focus on developing the talent of a select small group in your company and instead focus on lifting the talents of everyone in your organization. You need all of your team members doing their best to achieve your desired outcomes, so investing in each of them makes sense. Doing so also communicates to them they are each important to you, not just those "chosen" as high potential.

❖ Re-tool feedback and recognition. Evaluate and improve your feedback and recognition programs. Employees who do not feel their contributions are recognized are not motivated to do their best and quickly leave the organization. Or, worse, they stay with your organization occupying space and drawing a paycheck without rendering full effort.

❖ Measure and increase employee engagement. Measure your employee engagement annually, communicate the results to all employees, and act on the areas they indicate are lacking. Celebrate and amplify the areas they indicate are working.

❖ Deconstruct time and place. Evaluate and introduce where and when work is performed in your organization. In other words, consider hybrid or remote options and flexible schedules to accommodate the individual needs and desires of today's workforce desiring work-life harmony.

❖ Elevate your team by leveraging AI and robotics. Relieve the mundane tasks of your workforce with AI and robotics in a thoughtful way, focusing on how to elevate humanity in the workplace while staying true to your company purpose.

This chapter challenged you to consider likely long-held business and people management practices that seriously hamper the motivation and creativity of your team. Take stock of your organization and identify your opportunities for improvement by completing the checklist below. Indicate your rating of each practice in your organization as follows:

1 – Never

2 – Rarely

3 – Sometimes

4 – Most of the Time

5 – Always

Elevated Practice	Description	1	2	3	4	5
Audit and overhaul your human capital processes	You conduct and examine, ideally with the help of an outside perspective, your human capital processes to discern their impact on your employees' productivity, engagement, and performance.					
Seek what's good and develop strengths	You have a set of cultural operations in place where your managers look for what to prize in individual team members and actively work to develop their strengths and grow their talents to increase their fulfillment and further leverage their contributions.					

Focus on ALL team members	You do not subscribe to segregating your team into "high performance" or "low performance" but rather devote development resources to everyone.					
Intentional feedback and recognition	You regularly provide feedback that encourages a desire to improve, and feedback that motivates greater performance and a desire to stay.					
Measure your team's engagement with work	You annually measure the level of engagement (which is indicative of fulfillment) of your employees and act on the results to constantly improve the employee experience.					
Re-work where and when work gets done	You examine and incorporate hybrid and/or virtual and flexible work schedules that enable your team to more meaningfully participate in working while enjoying a great work-life harmony and fulfillment.					
Consciously threaded-in AI and robotics	You automate routine functions and relieve monotony of these tasks while thoughtfully elevating the human contribution to work.					

7

0: Open the Heart (EQ)

I have worked with many leaders who are a little squeamish about the presence of and communication about emotions in the workplace. Yet, emotions are an essential part of human nature. You and your team have a tremendous capacity to expand your range of emotional intelligence, which includes self-awareness, self-management, social awareness, and relationship management skills. Developing these skills will pay handsome dividends not just in your own immediate personal life but also have a large-scale impact in your organization.

Before diving into this chapter, it is useful to distinguish the difference between feelings and emotions. Emotions originate in our subconscious and play out in the body. Feelings, on the other hand, originate in the brain and are mental associations and reactions to emotions. Feelings are also amplified by our personal experience, beliefs, and memories. A feeling is a mental indication of what is going on in your body when you have an emotion and it is influenced by how your brain perceives and assigns meaning to the emotion.[1]

For example, you may notice the emotion of fear welling up inside you as your strongest team member asks to have a meeting with you. Your body expresses that emotion with sweaty palms and an increased heart rate. The feeling associated with this fear may be dread that this star person you count on is coming to you to put in her notice. And go to work for your biggest competitor! And take all your trade secrets with her! Notice how you are making "sense" of her request to meet, which all started with the emotion of fear.

The feelings that result based on your interpretation stemming from that emotion of fear will determine how you interact with this employee when she comes into your office to talk. Acting on the story just narrated above, you may immediately charge at her in the meeting and make these accusations before she even has the chance to explain why she wanted to talk. You then may never learn the actual intent of the conversation – to pitch you a new idea to create a new product line. Quite a difference in relationship and outcome. Distinguishing feelings and emotion are important to continue building your emotional intelligence, which is the thread undergirding all the practices recommended in this chapter.

Starting with the importance of developing into a caring leader who celebrates everyone and their contribution, you will also learn how to "manage through meaning," which the subsequent sections will further elaborate and extend. This is an approach to managing people that focuses on activating meaning and purpose in everyday work to make tasks more fulfilling for the team. You'll learn how to inspire love in work, so people engage more deeply of themselves in their work and are fueled by doing so. Fear, which can be a great motivator, you will learn also shuts down connection and innovation, while discerning "bad" fear and how you can manage away from it. You'll be introduced to the tool of "job purposing" to help your people find ways to activate more meaning on their own during the course of the day. Finally, you will learn how to increase the relational connection in your company and department through improved acumen in diversity, equity, inclusion, and belonging, and some ways to communicate authentically in environmental, social, and governmental matters.

Become a Caring Leader Who Celebrates "Everyone Matters"

You know you matter to someone when you feel seen and heard by them. To accomplish this feat – of registering to someone that you "get" them – takes skill and learning to be fully present. It also requires a lot of care and is utterly worth the effort. I learned what being a caring leader looks like in practice and scale from Bob Chapman, the CEO of Barry-Wehmiller you were introduced to in the last chapter. Bob told me "empathic listening" is at the heart of the BW University, which is not focused on gaining greater productivity from its students but rather "to enhance their ability to touch people's lives and equip them to be successful with others both inside and outside Barry-Wehmiller."[2] Bob is frequently sought after to speak to audiences across the globe about his "everybody matters," caring approach to leadership.

How might your results be improved were you to adopt this caring mindset in your leadership? You can fold "care" into your everyday operations by following the advice of Roger Steinkruger, who you met in Chapter 6.[3] To encourage "heart-warming," as he calls it, he recommends placing three agenda items for each leadership meeting:

- Time of Reflection: a topic of inspiration for the team
- Time of Recognition: for people present to recognize and thank others for going above and beyond
- A Time of Sharing: for people to share new services, ideas, accomplishments, and the rest of the team to practice servant leadership (focused on empowering employees, putting their needs first, and developing them) and inspirational leadership (communicating worth and potential to employees while casting a compelling vision they want to live in).[4]

You are the leader and must go first – open your heart to your people, without expecting anything in return. When you can make your people feel bold and hopeful, connected to something greater than themselves (discussed more in Chapter 8), confident and empowered to make an impact, you can bring out their best by helping them believe they can be more, do more, and make more good things happen.[5] You will be amazed by the extraordinary talent and goodness right inside your own organization, just waiting to be activated. Ordinary people can do extraordinary things if you create the right culture and a sustainable business model.[6] It will be overwhelming and hugely inspiring, filling your heart with love and abundance. When your people recognize that you "see" them and genuinely care for them, they will share your same sentiment and reciprocate, which greatly aids in your efforts to radically enliven your business (while magnificently accomplishing the same for yourself).

Managing Through Meaning™

Your people will register higher levels of well-being and productivity when they learn to stoke their own meaning engine. By learning to access and activate the three chief sources of meaning discussed in Chapter 4 (and translated to passion, inspiration, and mindset), your team is equipped to elevate their own energy and fulfillment any time. You as their leader can be enormously agentic in helping your team members access their individual meaning pathways and thus elevate their consciousness and the quality of their lives. This process begins with your first tapping into the deeper meaning in your own work, then creating conditions that enable your people to search for meaning in theirs. Through your invitation and communication, you create favorable conditions in everyday matters where your team members are then enabled to become "moment hunters," savoring the meaning in the moment and enjoying the fueling fulfillment accompanied. This philosophy of creating "moment hunters" is informed by the concept of *ichigo ichie,* which roughly translates from Japanese to "what we are experiencing now will never happen again."[7] Thus, we must treasure the moment and let its goodness wash over us. When you create a culture that encourages "moment hunters" and communicate how each person contributes to the purpose or mission of your organization, you activate the meaning potential in your people and literally turn them on from the inside by igniting their intrinsic motivation. This is what it means to "manage through meaning."

Organizations cannot *provide* meaning to their staff members per se, they can only *create* an environment in which individuals can be their own prime movers in the meaning process. This is the basis of a meaning-anchored culture you need to create that encourages individuals within it to reach for their own potential and be responsible for their fulfillment and career growth while contributing passionately from their talents and purpose. An organization that stewards its meaning journey can flex and grow, with infinite possibility, while expanding its consciousness and connection and contribution to the universe and its co-evolution, a concept further discussed in Chapter 8, Wake the Soul.[8] This is your opportunity to elevate meaning and its access to increase your people's fulfillment and engagement, which will translate to higher productivity and retention.

Having facilitated training programs based in traditional managerial skills to help transition thousands of individual contributors to become managers over the years, I developed my own program called Managing Through Meaning™ and use it in my consulting today. The program teaches the essential practical skills managers need, such as setting expectations, removing obstacles, communicating feedback, and delegating to grow team members, and layers in the ability to create workplaces where meaning is accessible. It also includes nuanced skills anchored in emotional intelligence, such as communicating team members' worth and potential[9] and looking for ways to help them activate their individual sources of meaning (passion, inspiration, and mindset) to increase their intrinsic motivation and fulfillment, among other areas. You can immediately start applying these ideas now to develop the connection with your team members and deepen the meaning they experience.

Descending deeper into the Managing Through Meaning™ material and distinguishing its logotherapeutic approach from other traditional management training programs, the content also teaches managers to leverage the five circumstances in logotherapy where meaning is often encountered, something else for you to add to your current approach. They are:

- Truth: helping people discover a truth about themselves. This insight may be triggered by an experience or by something seen, heard, read, fantasized, or dreamed about; but the discovery must be theirs that you help evoke. It could be a new realization – *yes, that's the way I am, how I act.* From childhood on, we are prompted to put on masks to please, to hide real or imagined weakness, to protect ourselves from rejection. Getting a peek under our masks will give us a sense of meaning.

- Seeing choices: helping people see choices in situations, as limited as they may be. Despair comes from a sense of feeling trapped. But we have choices under all circumstances, choices about the things we can change and choices about our attitudes regarding those we cannot change. When you help people become aware of a choice of attitudes, which in turn opens meanings in situations of unavoidable suffering or difficult circumstances that by themselves are meaningless, you help them see alternatives and they are likely to find a way forward and thus feel empowered.

- Uniqueness: helping people become aware of their own uniqueness. When we feel replaceable – in a job or a relationship – life seems meaningless. You can help people realize and claim their uniqueness by pointing out the quality they bring to relationships and the unique way they perform in their talents. In those moments, we help them see how they are irreplaceable.

- Responsibleness: helping people realize they are response-*able* for everything in their lives helps them see themselves as empowered, capable, and resourceful individuals who can take on life's challenges and create a fulfilling life for themselves. It builds their foundation to take on more challenges and increases their confidence in themselves.

- Self-transcendence: helping people find meaning and purpose by communicating how their actions and contributions help others. When people are affirmed by making a difference to others, they find meaning.

Just as it is for individuals, tapping your uniqueness as an organization is critical to realizing its potential.

People know the experience of meaning, of their limbic brains being triggered, but they have a difficult time tying it to the tasks of their work. They do know, however, what it is not. And despite the fact that many organizations have well-articulated missions and visions, they don't trigger the employees' limbic brains, if they don't inspire eudaimonic happiness, they're missing the goal; to tap into the wellspring of commitment, creativity, and resourcefulness that meaningful work elicits.[10]

Learn to manage through meaning, and you will radically enliven your organization. The remaining sections of this chapter all build on ways to manage through meaning.

Bring Passion Back to the Workplace

Why not create a workplace of play? Where your team feel like they are on the playground again, joyfully creating masterpieces in the dirt, hopscotching in chalked squares on the pavement, and pretending to be "cops and robbers"? People across the world have lost their childlike playfulness and don't know how to regain it, nor how to discover and live their passion and purpose. They are "auditing" life, literally walking through life "dead,"[11] and robbing themselves of the fulfillment that accompanies meaningful and joyous contribution. You, equipped with the principles in this book, can help your people find and live their passion again. Take instruction from the Japanese concept of *ikigai*, which provides a framework for helping people understand who they really are and live a more meaningful life. At its center is the delightful collision of finding what you love, what you're talented at, what you can be paid for, and what the world needs.[12]

By encouraging your team members to pursue personal and organizational dreams and passions, you get happier, loyal employees as well as increased productivity and improved financial performance.[13] The more the workforce can learn to tap into and work from their passion, the more they are able to persevere and persist in their tasks. Think of the creativity and innovation you can unleash when you create an environment where your team members are enthusiastically working from their passion and dedication to it.

Finally, you can take example from Dr. Claudia Beeny, the Chief "Shineologist" of the House of Shine, who is on a mission to help people ages 9 to 99 really understand what makes them "shine."[14] She has spent more than 30 years working in education, igniting the energy and passion of others. After a successful career in higher education, Claudia left her role to launch the House of Shine, a non-profit that helps people discover what makes them unique and how to leverage their *Shine* for the good of their community. Claudia and her team write K-12 curriculum, develop teaching tools, facilitate school assemblies and leadership experiences, and provide custom workshops to people of all ages. The House of Shine curriculum includes a focus on helping people understand their strengths, hobbies, interests, and needs among other things, and you can incorporate these "shine" principles into your own talent management practices. Doing so will help you create a learning culture and provide a place where your team members can develop their career over the long haul. Imagine how your company would be enlivened if you embraced the House of Shine "Do" principles: Be present. Create. Use your strengths. Keep perspective. Realize the impact of little things. Bring out the best in others. Reject mediocrity. Be relentlessly passionate. Be accountable. Spread shine.

Inspire "Love in Work" and Spread Joy

I know from years of working in employee engagement assessment/consulting and researching meaning in work that "work" occurs as a "four-letter word," or punishment for original sin, for a lot of people. My perspective on the word, formed since waiting tables in my parents' restaurant starting at age 14, is that the word signifies the way humankind spends their lives by being of service to others. The reality for many people, though, is that the workplace is not a nurturing playground but rather a toxic one to be endured. The way toward inspiring "love in work"[15] and spreading joy is, like most things in leadership, to start with yourself. What do *you* love about your work? Get clear about that, declare it for yourself, and then share it with your team. When you the leader talk about love in your work, you invite people to consider the same question for themselves. In your interactions with others, you can then ask them, "What do you love about your work?" When they tell you, listen with everything you've got so you convey you "see," understand, and appreciate them.

Only you can animate your spirit, only you can bring love into your world of work. The same is true of your people. You as their leader can do much to create an environment where they feel free, encouraged, and appreciated, which then reinforces the notion of embracing love in work. Build a culture and set of practices where your managers are looking for ways to unleash love in work. How does infusing love into work help your organization? When people love their work, they feel stronger, perform better, and bounce back from challenges faster. In other words, it *pays* to find ways to encourage your team to love their work. When you encourage people to pursue that which they are passionate about, they are more likely to gain mastery over their tasks. Why is striving toward mastery important? Mastery is:

> About understanding your potential and then dedicating your life to pursuing that ideal. It means doing your absolute best. Why? Because the craft deserves it, because the calling requires it, and because maybe you'll be a better person for it. After all, this is the role of work in our lives – not only as a means to make a living, but as a tool to make us into who we were born to be.[16]

What would your organization look like if your people were enabled to become the best version of themselves *in your company,* doing the work you count on them performing, that leads them into the best version of themselves they can be? I dare say the energy generated would represent a seismic shift upwards from the culture you have today.

When we can experience love in work, it yields access to the emotion of joy, which is known to boost the immune system, reduce stress, and increase longevity. How can you help your team find joy in their work and lives? Let's look to another shining example as we did with passion and "shine." It was somewhere in June of 2019 when my phone rang and on the other end of it was a woman named Sheryl Lynn. She was driving from the Midwest to Oregon, where she planned to visit her daughter, and had caught on the road a recent *Working on Purpose* episode I'd hosted with Melerick Mitchell.[17] Mel and I had been conversing about the importance of infusing passion into one's career, just as was discussed in the previous section. For Sheryl Lynn, her purpose was ultimately recognized as that insistent calling toward anything that brought her joy. She understood to her core she *needed* it, and so does everyone else. And now she's built a platform around her brand called JOYELY and is stewarding a Joy Movement to serve one billion people as they find and share their joy with the world. I have found my own joy in encouraging Sheryl along her journey to make it a way of life for everyone.

You have a tremendous opportunity in your organization to help your team members activate their joy. Joy positively *infects* people. Invite people to share what brings them joy, whether at work or elsewhere, to increase their vibrational energy for themselves *and* enable them to positively infect those witnessing the share. Why not integrate a regular practice to invite your team members to share what brings them joy, and why? How about kicking off your regular meetings with an invitation from the team to share what has recently brought them joy? Bonus: when you listen to your team member express what brings them joy, you learn who they are and what matters to them. And then when you, the leader, recognize and appreciate them for who they are and for what they shared, you create a connection between you, the person who shares, and the rest of the team that is "sticky," that unites and fortifies the team.

Stomp Out Fear and Toxicity

My consulting experience has taught me that most leaders inside organizations have no idea how much fear exists in and runs their operations, creating a toxic environment and diminishing connection and productivity. Getting away from a toxic environment is one of the factors fueling the Great Resignation – people are seeking a healthy place to work and grow their careers. "Fear is the single biggest source of waste in organizations today. At the same time, it is the least understood, most neglected, and most dramatically underestimated issue in modern organizational life."[18] Are *you* aware of the extent of fear's existence in your organization? You would be the rare person if you were fully aware of the presence and potency of fear among your team members. Fear is something many organizations don't like to talk about, and many leaders don't want to admit to feeling, as there is a belief it connotes weakness, failure, or that you don't believe you can handle the demands of your role.[19]

A critical aspect to know about this human emotion: fear is contagious. "Once fear becomes a mood or a habit for one person in an organization, that mindset can quickly spread. This is because humans, as deeply social beings, mirror the emotions and behaviors of the people around them."[20] "All this fear seeps into the very DNA of an organization. Once there, it silently and insidiously drives dysfunction in every aspect of the organization: strategy, operations, cross-functional collaboration, human capital management, team dynamics, employee engagement, and employee well-being."[21]

Here's how to recognize fear in your organization so you can intervene to stop the behaviors feeding it. Fear manifests in the experience of a boss who is verbally abusive, of losing a job, of asserting oneself or speaking up, of pushing back on unreasonable expectations, of public speaking, of asking for a promotion, of sharing new ideas, of being shut down, of being undermined by a coworker, of being an imposter, of being lonely, of "staying stuck," of change, of being adventurous, and of failure. What's more, living in a nonstop state of fear can cause unwanted physical effects, such as increased heart rate and lower oxygen levels.

Allowing bullies to exist in your organization compounds fear and creates a toxic environment that paralyzes productivity and innovation and sends your people marching for the exits. Bullying shows up as threats, degradation or humiliation, mean-spirited pranks, and angry, aggressive, and condescending language. You'll also recognize it when someone repeatedly picks apart another's work, they withhold information or sabotage someone else's work, or there is social exclusion or isolation.[22] Your job in creating a meaning-anchored workplace is to constantly hold vigilance of the mood of your workplace and be on the lookout for any of these tell-tale signs of bullying. The moment you notice it, immediately and privately confront the person and do not tolerate it. I have been called into various companies over the years by leaders wanting "professional development" for their team, when in fact they hoped to deal with a single bully who was polluting the whole team though lacked the communication expertise or courage to confront them.

The first step is to recognize that fear exists in your company[23] – and determine its source and how it manifests itself in behavior. Fear is natural in the business world, where leaders continually worry about losing out to the competition or making a crucial mistake. The key is to have the right balance of fear in motivating yourself and others, and not to let your fears bring out the worst in you or your team members.[24] This exercise is not about removing fear or denying it, but rather transforming your relationship to it. Authors Bhatnagar and Minukas offer the imperative to "unfear" your organization, and distinguish that "unfear" is not the opposite of fear, nor is it a synonym for fearless. To "unfear" is to reframe the experience of fear so that you can first free yourself of reactive patterns to it and gain mastery over your response to make different choices. Through this reframing exercise, you can enable a state of being in which you welcome fear as an opportunity to learn while unleashing a higher performance in yourself, team, and ultimately the full organization. It means shifting the story you carry within yourself about fear and seeing the learning that fear can offer everyone.[25]

As fear is a natural motivator, it can be harnessed in a healthy way to unleash higher performance. Just as the concept of "good stress" or "eustress" is seen to motivate, "eufear" or "positive fear" can provide a positive cognitive response to stress that is healthy and provide a sense of focus and fulfillment in the effort the fear motivates.[26] A complete lack of fear, where it's perceived there is nothing at stake to lose, results in people not taking risks or exercising initiative. When fear is present, your opportunity is to recognize that underneath all fears are deeper underlying emotions and unmet needs. Your job is to uncover these emotions for yourself to become the most effective leader you can be, and then learn to help your team members do the same. John Baird and Edward Sullivan, executive coaches and co-authors, have developed a simple framework to help you manage your fears by:

- naming your fear and embracing it;
- sharing your fear with a coach or colleague;
- making a plan to choose different behaviors;
- narrating your fear through storytelling.[27]

Storytelling is an effective way to normalize fear in your organization. One of the most effective ways you can turn fear into an ally is to openly – and vulnerably – share the fear you're feeling with your team or organization. Sharing your story can be a powerful step to embracing your fear and sparking conversations about fear with others. Baird and Sullivan recite a powerful story in their book about a CEO they worked with who shared with his full team his fear of not making the necessary financial numbers to keep the company afloat. This executive went on to say that he did not have the answers but was confident he had the right people in the room to help solve the problem and that they could come through together. He told them just how much was at stake – his own investment, the loss of the company, their jobs. Every eye and heart was riveted on this leader, and the authors go on to report that the team ultimately pulled together and turned the company around.[28] I witnessed a similar situation when a leader I was working with to steward an ambitious new global product launch in a consumer packaging organization opened his kick-off speech with the promise of the initiative right alongside his own fears of the magnitude of what they were embarking on. There were 60 people working on that project, and over the course of the months working together, they leaned in, and scoured for ways to move the initiative across the finish line. And did!

Fear, used honestly, wisely, and productively, works. The most unproductive or hurtful behaviors you experience in others are often motivated by fear. Get curious and try to see the fear behind the actions that hurt you, and then you have a better chance of resolving the conflict without being triggered into fear yourself.[29] Develop the capacity to do this for yourself, and then enable your team to do the same by making it safe to talk openly about fear and how to productively leverage it.

Encourage Social or Job Purposing

We all have day-to-day tasks, some of which delight and others we dread. "Yet no matter what occupies our days, when we *reframe* our tasks as opportunities to help others, our lives and our work feel more significant... that's a legacy everyone can leave behind."[30] Even to simply reframe tasks as opportunities to help other people can make life and work feel more meaningful. You and your team members can even learn to "sneak in" creative ways to help people during the course of your work days, something Bea Boccalandro refers to as job purposing or social purposing.

> Job purposing is any meaningful contribution to others or to a societal cause done as part of our work experience. Put another way, job purposing is a work-related action that, from the point of view of the individual performing it, furthers social purpose.[31]

What does that look like at work? Boccalandro provides the example of a parking lot attendant infusing social purpose into his workday. By making it a practice to measure the tread of the tires on the cars he parks and alert the owners when they are wearing dangerously thin, he knows he is averting potential disaster along the highway when the tires would otherwise blow. He is thanked profusely by the appreciative, and often surprised, car owners who are stunned and delighted by the completely unexpected "extra" service and care lavished upon them.[32] This example represents a simple intervention of task but large payoff in meaning and fulfillment for the parking attendant. It's also an illustration of how conscious intentionality in pursuit of an overall meaningful life affords the bounty treasure side effect of well-being. Well-being has been identified as a core initiative inside organizations, especially since the beginning of the COVID-19 pandemic, and the Gallup Organization, long known for its intense focus on employee engagement, has released a new book called *Well-Being at Work: How to Build Resilient and Thriving Teams.*[33] Boccalandro continues:

> The practice of doing good at work is how we get beyond bringing only a fractured version of ourselves

to work. It's how we banish the chronic ache of our unmet longing for meaningful work. Infusing our work with social purpose is nothing less than a path to restoring the whole of who we are.[34]

One way to surface purpose in your organization is to ask your team members to share how what they do in their job makes a difference or matters to others. To illustrate by example, Zach Mercurio shares a wonderful story about the Economics of Mattering. Some years ago, KPMG set out on an informational campaign seeking 10,000 stories about how their work mattered from 27,000 employees. The result? They received over a whopping 40,000![35] The potential was always there – the company only needed to summon it and then enjoy the crescendo of positive energy doing so unleashed. Start by asking your team members how their work matters, or how they snuck in a way to help someone outside their regular duties. Consider how their doing so gave them access to vital meaning through self-transcendence *and* may even have created goodwill for your organization in the process.

Socialize the idea of job purposing through your managers to encourage it in their teams. Teach the managers, who coach their team members, why social purposing is important to your organization and illustrate how it creates the culture you desire (because mattering *matters*). Some ways you and your managers can encourage social purposing include tilting a task toward social purpose like the parking attendant did and promoting equity or supporting others in issues important to them. Helping coworkers with their work and practicing environmental sustainability with your company are additional ways your team members can practice social purpose and reap the benefits. The bottom line is, if people don't feel their jobs improve the world, enable and empower them to improve their jobs through social purpose.

Increase Relational Connection and Belonging Through DEIB

Think back to when you were a kid – was there ever a time when you were the last one picked for a team or a school project? It's a lonely, alienating feeling – to think that no one really wants you to work with them or play with them. Sure, your school or team may have made it mandatory that everyone be included, but that doesn't mean someone wasn't picked last. And the kid picked last knows that others don't really want him or her. They know that the others are required to include them. That's not acceptance – it's just compliance. What an awful, uncomfortable, self-conscious feeling this experience conjures. For many people of color, this is daily life. Made to feel last. Less than. Different. Unwanted.[36]

At work, what must it feel like to be the only one, or the one left out of the group, or the one who is grudgingly accepted, but only because the others must comply? Develop the skills to embrace diversity, which includes tolerance for others different than ourselves and respect for those differences. DEIB is where it's at today – diversity, equity, inclusion, and now, *belonging*. People don't perform well when they don't feel seen, understood, or belong. You're committed to making your team or your company better for diverse employees, and, especially if you're White, it starts with flexing your own empathy muscle and thinking about what work must feel like for people of color. In the words of Stephen R. Covey and his daughter Cynthia Covey Haller:

> [P]eople are extremely tender inside, particularly those who act as if they are tough and self-sufficient. We must listen to them with the "third-ear," the heart. We can gain even greater influence with them by showing love, particularly unconditional love, which gives people a sense of intrinsic worth and security without enforcing behavior or comparisons with others.[37]

Articles, books, training, and classes on Diversity, Equity, Inclusion, and Belonging are important and necessary.

> But if you're White and you listen to someone of another race or background describe their first-hand, personal day-to-day experiences, it's incredibly eye opening. The terrible things that happen to Black, Brown, Asian, LGBTQ+, Jewish, Amish, and Muslim (or any minority group) people just don't typically happen to Whites.[38]

We (speaking as a white woman) can't imagine how bad it is, or how often it happens, and we can't comprehend the chronic toll it takes on a person. As the leader, you set the standard for how DEIB is lived in your company. Wherever you are in the journey, talking about your people's differences is key. You can start by situating the discourse with something like this:

> It's in our best interest to make sure that everyone in this department (or team or company) has equal opportunity to learn, grow, and advance profession- ally. We need to have regular, ongoing conversations about race and inequity at work, so that we can ad- dress the things we do that aren't working and come up with new solutions.[39]

Considering the changing demographics, your efforts to make everyone in your organization feel they belong and matter becomes even more compelling. As of 2021, "the Latinx/Hispanic population in the United States is 19% of the total population, and the black population is 14%. That's a full third of the US population! It would be foolish to ignore a third of the market, but many businesses do."[40] If you have trouble finding or keeping people of color as employees, it's wise to inquire and consider whether your work environment isn't as welcoming or as comfortable as you think. You may also be missing out on opportunities to innovate or compete more competitively without sufficient diversity in your organization. With only one lens on the way you and your team view business, you squander the benefit of other perspectives that might challenge your thinking, create better solutions, or offer new ideas. The way forward is not to pretend, nor to create a color-blind workplace. If you pretend to ignore skin color or dismiss it entirely, you minimize and negate the prejudice, bias, and racism that people of color experience. The goal is to create a more equitable and inclusive workplace, and we can only do that when we acknowledge our differences and work to create a level playing field for everyone. This is about creating an environment that magnetizes everyone to want to connect, perform, feel they belong, and are part of something bigger that benefits the world, which will be addressed in more detail in Chapter 8, Wake the Soul.

Live the ESG+R Standard Every Day

Aiming to make a difference in the world beyond earning healthy profits is good for the health and vitality of all your company's stakeholders. The world has so many problems and opportunities awaiting a motivated workforce to take on. Employees know when they're part of a great organization, something they're proud of that enlarges them, and they dig deep to apply their efforts to perform higher and vie to remain part of such an organization. Anaplan CEO Frank Calderoni talks about how the trifecta of unexpected events no one could have expected of the global pandemic, recession, and murder of George Floyd (and now the Russia-Ukraine war) has heightened expectations that employees, customers, and investors have of the business sector to lead the way through daily change. Not only that, but stakeholders are holding companies accountable for societal, governmental, and environmental practices with little tolerance for inaction, as discussed in Chapter 3, Sustainability in an Interdependent World.

What does this heightened awareness and accountability mean for you as a leader? Calderoni puts forth that company character is the core that grounds culture and strategy and is the throughline of fundamental beliefs and values that unite people and teams working with a shared purpose. He says company character comprises the qualities and behaviors that define people – such things as empathy, courage, authenticity, integrity, honesty, and respect. And those things are embodied in how you work every day, treat others, and treat yourself. These attributes combine to create positive interactions and relationships that your stakeholders recognize and reward you with loyalty, engagement, and goodwill, Calderoni says. Your company character is measured by the distance between what you say and do. He says that organizations that internalize and live and demonstrate upstanding company character in every action are the organizations that will win today and in the future. The bottom line is that people make decisions on what to buy, where to work, whom to partner, and whom to affiliate with or invest in based on a company's values and the character displayed by its people.

What does this mean for you as a leader? It means you can't afford to be silent on matters at large as they relate to your values.

Recall the story in Chapter 3 when Coca-Cola took a stand on Atlanta's initial unwillingness to recognize Dr. Martin Luther King's Nobel Peace prize. This example showcases not just the need for business leaders like you to take a stand on ESG+R (environmental, social, governance, and resilience) issues, but also the sheer positive impact on social justice you can have through your organizational reputation and resources. Moreover, as Calderoni asserts, you can no longer remain silent on racial justice or sustainability. When you are silent on issues that matter, people will fill in the gaps themselves – and most likely negatively. If you don't convey and demonstrate your support for diversity and inclusion, then top candidates will pass you by – looking for employers that do. If you don't talk about your stance on climate change, they'll assume you don't care about climate change, when very likely you do. This is especially true in crises, as they reveal what your company and its people are really made of. Let me be very clear: you will lose some stakeholders when you speak your position on ESG+R matters, and you will absolutely gain others who fervently align with you. Not taking a stand, though, diminishes your credibility and relationships, which again is no longer being tolerated by employees and customers. Better to take your organizational position, in relation to your values and purpose, and stand and speak from there.

Key Points Summary

❖ Become a caring leader who celebrates "everyone matters". When you behave and communicate to show your care and appreciation for each person on the team and show them how they matter, you activate powerful meaning that compels people to give their best and want to stay.

❖ Manage through meaning. Activate meaning by intentionally incorporating ways in everyday interactions for people to experience the three sources of meaning in logotherapy of passion, inspiration, and mindset.

❖ Bring passion back to the workplace. As passion is one of the three sources of meaning available in logotherapy, help your people discover their passions and then continue developing them, both inside your workplace and beyond. Passionate people are energized and positively infect others with their radiant energy, elevating the vitality of the whole team.

❖ Inspire "love in work" and spread joy. Helping your people to spend most of their day doing tasks they love rather than those that drain them is an excellent and immediate remedy to the disengagement problem. Modeling and encouraging your team to find and express joy is both positively intoxicating as well as a boost to well-being.

❖ Stomp out fear and toxicity. Fear in organizations is an absolute productivity and connection killer, and it's rampant and often left to run unchecked, creating a toxic environment. One of the reasons people seek a different job is to relieve themselves of this toxicity. Your job as the leader is to keep a constant pulse on the emotional heartbeat in your workplace and to immediately intervene when anyone, especially managers, operate in ways that induce fear. People are often not aware of the ramifications of their actions and communication, so you must call out the behavior (privately) and address the behavior change with professional development.

❖ Encourage social or job purposing. The experience of any job can be elevated by modeling and encouraging your team members to look for ways to help others through the normal course of everyday operations. Build this mentality into your culture and you also further elevate a mindful stakeholder service tactic that fortifies the heartbeat of your people while also caring for your community and elevating your reputation.

❖ Increase relational connection through DEIB. Creating an environment where people feel they matter and belong is essential to thriving and remaining relevant in today's times. The world is increasingly diverse and living the diversity, equity, inclusion, and belonging standard takes commitment to steward and hold everyone accountable to uphold it.

❖ Live the ESG+R standard every day. People expect companies and their leaders to be mindful, vigilant, and active in their words and actions on ESG matters. They seek to join companies that align with their own environmental and social values, and they monitor the governance practices of companies in alignment with those values. Leaders cannot be silent on ESG and resiliency matters as doing so sends the unintended message they do not care about them.

This chapter encouraged you to "open the heart" to increase emotional intelligence and manage through meaning to increase motivation and connection among your team members. Take stock of your organization and identify your opportunities for improvement by completing the checklist below. Indicate your rating of each practice in your organization as follows:

1 – Never

2 – Rarely

3 – Sometimes

4 – Most of the Time

5 – Always

Elevated Practice	Description	1	2	3	4	5
Become a caring leader	We operate from a culture that prizes the worth and potential of each team member and convey this message through words and deeds.					

Manage through meaning	We traffic in meaning by incorporating ways for people to experience daily somehow the three sources of meaning in logotherapy – passion, inspiration, and mindset.					
Bring passion back	We celebrate passion by helping team members discover their own, develop it with and through their work, and encourage its pursuit beyond the workplace.					
Inspire "love in work"	We continually seek ways to keep our team members focused on doing work they most enjoy, properly aligning their time and talents with their treasure.					
Stomp out fear and toxicity	We do not tolerate fear to manifest toxically in our operations and actively intervene to mobilize "eufear" to unleash productivity through authenticity and vulnerability.					
Encourage job purposing	We live the job purposing mantra by modeling it in our own work and recognizing and celebrating it through the efforts of our team members.					

Increase relational connection through DEIB	We constantly seek to recognize and understand the natural differences that emerge in a diverse culture by openly discussing them and soliciting ideas from the full population in the organization how to include, recognize, leverage and appreciate those differences.					
Live the ESG+R standard	We take a stand on ESG+R matters and communicate our position publicly and within the company to be transparent and attract and keep those stakeholders who align with us.					

8

W: Wake the Soul (SQ)

As you've come this far in the book you know that your people crave meaningful work, and you have a tremendous playground through which to offer it to them in your organization. Opportunity is ripe for you to help your team members more fully awaken and activate their meaning and purpose potentials through an enlightened, conscious lens – the one you'll be further learning about in this chapter. Embracing the lessons in this book and putting them into practice will enable you to unleash a "deliberately developmental organization."[1] Now that you are familiar with practices to develop and transform your organization based in IQ and EQ principles, from Chapters 6 and 7, respectively, we can now turn to the next frontier, SQ, or spiritual intelligence, to enhance your capacity to lead from inspiration and guide your organization into a magnanimous future.

Humans are irreducibly spiritual creatures, a perspective Viktor Frankl has long touted but that has only recently gained visage in today's business world. Similarly, "soul" is steadily emerging in business, and Wolfe reports in his book *The Living Organization* that companies such as Nokia, Unilever, McKinsey, Shell, Coca-Cola, Hewlett Packard, Merck Pharmaceuticals, and Starbucks are using models for developing and measuring spiritual intelligence.[2]

A soul in the business sense can be defined as "the vital force behind the animating activities that brings the entity to life."[3] Moreover, "I believe it is a mistake, if not simply selling ourselves short, to leave *soul* out of our conversations around business. The invisible forces that animate us and bond us are worthy of direct infusion into the discussion and practices of our work."[4] The promise of this chapter speaks to your role as a leader to steward the consciousness journey in your organization and lead deeply from purpose and elevate the humanity among all your stakeholders. Morris situates the opportunity to simultaneously draw from and elevate our full complement of intelligence in this passage:

> Among the truest parts to our humanity is that we are paradoxical. We have the unique ability to hold multiple simultaneous truths together. We are part primal animal tethered to the natural world and part soul-filled beings animated by unseen forces. We are part cooperative beings that shape the world around us and part imaginative beings that envision a future. We are part dreamer, part maker, part security seeker, part possibility creator.[5]

This chapter invites you to step further into the realm of this "both/and" paradigm for yourself and on behalf of your organization by providing seven best practices to further elevate spiritual intelligence in your organization. By now, you know the journey starts with *you* – there is no substitute for doing the hard work to become and remain the leader worth following. To be an effective leader in today's purpose economy, learning to add an inspirational component enables you to influence and impact more deeply and effectively. Detecting and articulating your company's reason for being as clear purpose, mission, and vision statements communicates the inspiring vision you are out to realize, together, as a team. Your team members will want in on that action, and when you help them discover their own purpose and align it with and through your company's, you radically improve their lives and the very spiritual health of your company. To maintain the momentum you create achieving these efforts, inculcating "deep purpose" into your culture and operations is the glue that makes it all stick. You can draw from the four-part transformation model I created and use in my consulting to get you started while you move toward adding in beauty to elevate your business model, which will both inspire you as well as attract hearts and minds passionate about what you stand to accomplish. Finally, you'll finish this chapter by exploring ways to reach for your own higher potential and that of your team members.

Do the Work – Be a Leader Worth Following

Wherever your organization is along the evolution and maturation trajectory, you have ongoing work to do on yourself. The level of maturity and consciousness your company exhibits are a direct reflection of your own as the leader or owner. In other words, the organization you lead cannot evolve past your own level of consciousness. You are the stop gap. "Unevolved leaders hold the business back from realizing its potential. Evolving leaders keep the flow of forward growth and allow the business to keep flourishing."[6]

Effective leadership starts with doing your own work on yourself to understand who you are and how your words and actions impact the team. Your level of evolution as a person is the most significant determinator of your effectiveness as a leader. "When underdeveloped people lead us, their lack of wholeness affects us as followers. And when we follow leaders who have done the hard work of becoming whole people, we feel that as well."[7] Only when leaders have done their important self-work can they employ the dynamic trio of grit, grace, and gravitas, which speaks to perseverance, emotional intelligence, and competence, respectively, as Jane Firth and Andrea Zintz[8] so eloquently state.

It is likely you do not fully comprehend the impact, both positive and negative, you have on those you lead. Your work on yourself as a leader is never complete and will require your ongoing self-inquiry to understand your own preferences for communicating and behaving, and your ongoing enrollment in courses, programs, and coaches to continue your own development and steward your consciousness journey. Tim Spiker and his team at Aperio are dedicated to help people become, be, and remain leaders who are worth following. When I asked him on air about where his deep passion came from, he told me a story of an experience he had working for a terrible leader some years prior.[9] He recounted how working for this leader not only left him feeling depleted and deflated, but the experience was also negatively cascaded onto others. By that, he meant he often came home after a full day of work and complained about his day for more than an hour to his wife, who thus also fell victim to the negative shrapnel this unevolved leader shot through the people in his organization.

That experience helped shape Spiker's passion and resolve to help develop leaders worth following who are "inwardly sound" and "others focused," and stop the poisoning of those who have yet to do the necessary work on themselves. This too is your task – to become "inwardly sound" and "others focused." Spiker says, "Being out of touch with the reality of our own (especially negative) impact as leaders is one of the most egregious forms of leadership failure we can commit."[10] Spiker distinguishes the who and what of leadership and purports that three-quarters of your effectiveness as a leader comes from *who* you are, not *what* you do. Let that sobering truth sink in. *Who* you are dictates *what* you do. How does this personal development and evolution of you the leader impact the bottom line? Spiker says his team used data from anonymous assessments on CEOs to evaluate their integrity, responsibility, forgiveness, and compassion, and then compared each organization's financial performance. They found that the bottom 10 CEOs had a return on assets of 1.93% while the top 10 CEOs with the highest measure of those qualities had a 9.35% ROA.[11]

The sooner and higher you aim to develop your capacity to live in and activate the full complement of your intellect, senses, and spirituality, the greater your company can soar. This may sound daunting to you, but it's spot on. "The leader is the most emotionally influential person in the room. We must be conscious of this if we are to be leaders worth following." As Spiker says, an unexamined life is not worth following. To be effective in today's extremely demanding business environment, you need to be able to answer that question – are you worth following?[12] "Evolved leaders are driven by and connected to a higher purpose and vision, who know that becoming the best leader they can be is an upward-spiral process they will never fully complete."[13]

As a leader, you are the beacon source and example for the rest of the organization. It does not matter how successful you have been to date, you must put in the work to understand yourself and your impact on others, and to improve your relational EQ and SQ capacities. Commit to becoming an evolved leader – one who is traveling a committed path to the continuous growth and evolution of yourself and for those around you – a path that considers and manages the interconnected nature of the beliefs, systems, processes, and multiple stakeholders in and around the business.

Raj Sisodia and Michael Gelb describe in *The HEALING Organization* four essential energies that leaders must awaken to elevate their consciousness and ultimately heal themselves. These energies manifest as:

- tough-minded (masculine);
- tenderhearted (feminine);
- wise and connected to your principled wise higher selves (elder);
- playful, retaining our joyful, healthy child energy (child).[14]

Carefully choose leadership development programs and participate in learning activities every year, specifically those that help you develop the above characteristics offered by Spiker and Sisodia and Gelb. Secure and work with an executive coach who will help illuminate your blind spots and provide alternative ways to relate to people and address problems while communicating possibility through your vision. The *Vitally Inspired* leadership program I created and offer inside companies is another option. It is designed to awaken your passion and purpose and transform you into an inspirational leader who communicates worth and invites followers to work toward their potential.

Purpose has become not a question of *if* but rather to *what* level you and your organization are living it. Dr. Holly Woods has written a captivating book called *The Golden Thread* in which she maps 12 levels of consciousness to their associative purpose expression. She hypothesizes that the type of purpose one experiences is likely related to their developmental stage. The higher the level of development, the greater the expression and impact of purpose. To fully understand the opportunity to express through purpose, and to try to discern your own level of purpose development along the 12 levels, her book is a great start.[15] She says, "We are evolutionary beings – always birthing another version of our essential beingness. In this way, we are also always birthing another version of our purpose – one that is more expressive and integrates all of us or that transcends and includes all that came before."[16] While it may seem daunting to consider the depth and breadth of self work necessary to become your most effective as a leader, I hope you also recognize the immense opportunity to realize your own potential and express your highest purpose in doing so.

Add Inspiration to Evolve Your Leadership Practice

I believe the most effective leaders are inspirational, and my first book in fact is titled *Purpose Ignited: How Inspiring Leaders Unleash Passion and Elevate Cause*. I'm in good company with other well-established leaders and teachers of leadership who agree. Dr. Lance Secretan, who you met in the Foreword to this book, is one of them. Having served early in his career as the Managing Director of Manpower, which employed 72,000 full- and part-time employees, he went on to teach leadership at university level, has written 24 books on leadership, and now consults with large organizations on their business issues. The silver bullet to being an effective leader, he says? Exactly, you know it – INSPIRATION.[17]

My experience has further taught me that you cannot become an inspirational leader until you've accessed your own soul to know and appreciate yourself, activated your passion and inspiration, and want to serve others. By "soul," I align with Dr. Arthur Ciaramicoli's definition, which is "the invisible, intangible part of every human being that yearns for attachment to something deeper and broader than what we perceive to be ourselves."[18] Being an inspirational leader first requires that you tap into, live and express that which lights you up from inside, and then communicate the worth and potential of your people in such a compelling fashion they cannot resist reaching toward the vision you cast of them. People know on a "visceral, emotional level when someone has soul," and they feel elevated and energized by it – which is a big part of why being an inspirational leader is so effective.[19]

You don't need a charismatic personality to be inspirational, though it can increase your impact. What is necessary is to be authentic about who you are at your core, so people feel they know you, and then learn to be a powerful storyteller painting the future of your organization. How do you access the source of inspiration? As unsavory as it may sound, you are well positioned to navigate this path when you have experienced some kind of awakening or turning point. Often, these awakening experiences occur while confronting such serious life circumstances as divorce, disaster, death, or some version of a failure. Your reception, reaction, and navigation through these events determines who you become as a result. Embracing them as key teaching moments, and adopting what Morris calls an "evolving leader" approach, allows you to emerge more committed and more lucid in your understanding of why you're here and what you'll do with your life. You can also travel the "evolving leader" path through a contemplative path of processing and introspection derived from the deep reflection of your life experiences and how they reveal your essence and what is meaningful to you.[20] No matter what, the journey toward becoming an evolved, inspirational leader takes real work, and the results are proportionate to the work you put in.

What does an inspirational leadership look like in practice? In a conversation with Roger Steinkruger, the healthcare CEO you met in previous chapters, he shared just how much he learned from Dr. Secretan as he took part in his leadership programs over the years.[21] His own book is inspired by and adapted from Secretan's philosophy of inspiration being a key motivational force.[22] Steinkruger's advice to put inspiration into practice is to make it a habit to inspire others to be the best they are capable of being. This takes proactively looking for their gifts and helping them see possibilities in themselves they may not otherwise see for themselves. He goes on to insist you become a risk-taker and invest in practicing as an inspiring, loving, and servant leader not just because this is the best use of your time as a leader, but also because the personal and professional rewards are endless. Steinkruger says, after all, "what can be more gratifying than to personally witness others blooming where they are planted? What can be better for business than improving productivity, reducing turnover, and improving the bottom line?"[23] I have personally benefitted from an inspirational leader I was incredibly fortunate enough to have at age 19 who saw possibilities in me I could *never* have envisioned for myself. It is due to his articulated vision of me and kicking me out of his company in my first job out of high school that I earned a PhD, lived abroad, and have lived a completely different life than the smaller one I envisioned for myself.

In the final tally,

> What we, as team members, want from you our team leader, is firstly that you make us feel part of something bigger, that you show us how what we are doing together is important and meaningful; and secondly, that you make us feel that you can see us, and connect to us, and care about us, and challenge us, in a way that recognizes who we are as individuals. We ask you to give us this sense of universality – all of us together – and at the same time to recognize our own uniqueness; to magnify what we all share, and to lift up what is special about each of us.[24]

I can't say it better than that. Serving as an inspirational leader requires you first tuning in and being turned on by your own life. It is from that place you can better see what is special and magical in others, what their gifts are. As Steinkruger says, to be great at this, you need to learn to really see your people for the unique souls they are and love them for it. In short, you need "the Grinch experience" – where a lifetime misanthrope is transformed by a near-death fall down a snowy mountain at Christmastime. To get the full picture and learn the lesson, your assignment is to rent and watch *How the Grinch Stole Christmas*.[25]

Detect Your Company's Purpose – Your Unique Way of Being and Serving

Whether your organization has been in existence for 25 years, or 25 months, it's likely you and your team members lack a clear idea of its purpose. Why does it exist, and why should anyone care? It's important for people in companies to work out their "house of meaning" together, rather than have it assigned and pushed down into the organization, which renders meaningless that which was intended to be meaningful.[26] Calderoni and I agree that purpose must be generated from the bottom up in an organization, which requires enrolling all team members in its discovery and articulation. I quite align with what Gulati shared of LEGO's former CEO and now Chairman of the Board, Knudstorp. "If you want to transform – not just turn around – a company," Knudstorp observed,

> [Y]ou need to find the essence of the brand, your unique identity... finding that identity is just like finding out your purpose in life – it's not up to you, not up to management, to decide that. It's not a rational choice. You don't "decide" what your calling is. You *detect* it.[27]

In the process, you are looking to discover elements of the early business that, articulated in the form of a purpose statement, might continue to inspire, animate, and guide people toward the future, giving the organization meaning and a sense of having been chosen for an important mission. Your deliverable in the purpose expedition process, in conjunction with the active participation of your team, is to derive inspiring statements for your organization that describe each of the following:

1) Your company's purpose: Why does your organization exist, and why should anyone care?
2) Your mission: What product or service does your organization provide in service to its purpose; how are you distinguished in its delivery?
3) Your vision: What does the world look like in the future when your organization has fully executed its purpose?
4) Values: The principles that govern how your organization does what it does qualitatively.

In defining purpose, it helps to look further to the past, deeply investigating the intentions of the founders and early employees,

> scouring for themes that capture the firm's ineffable soul or essence. This attention to history lends purpose an extra weightiness, resulting in deeper emotional connections and more commitment to the reason for being. Paradoxically, it also serves as a bridge to the future, helping [you] to chart a path ahead that is meaningful, coherent, and grounded.[28]

These statements should be deeply inspiring and completely accurate. "When this 'why' is defined, written down, and put into action throughout the organization, it exponentially enlarges its impact."[29] These statements serve to communicate what you stand for and thus invite those similarly dispositioned and repel those who do not align. When you (and your team) write your purpose statement, make it more compelling by including two basic and interrelated features. First, be sure to delineate an ambitious, longer-term goal for your company. Second, give this goal an idealistic cast, one that commits your organization to the fulfillment of broader social duties.[30]

As purpose can be elusive to discover and articulate, it is often helpful to work with a guide or facilitator who is skilled in eliciting responses from you and the team as to your company's purpose. In my consulting firm, we use a four-step model I developed to help organizations move through a desired transformation outcome, including the detection and expression of purpose (see Table 1).

Table 1 Alise Cortez and Associates Model of Transformation

Symptoms	Interventions	Results
PHASE 1 – ENLIVEN		
Lackluster business results Low employee engagement Poor employee performance High attrition Little to no innovation	Purpose and Culture interview, assessment, analysis	Results presentation with team to refine and align on Purpose, Mission, Vision statements, and surface cultural and operational improvement opportunities.
PHASE 2 – ENLIGHTEN		
Leadership team is motivated to address issues learned in Phase 1 assessment to improve business operations.	People process audit is performed to evaluate effectiveness and seek ways to better "humanize" the employee experience: recruitment, onboarding, training, promotion, recognition, etc.	Company has vital intelligence with actionable recommendations to improve the full employee experience and create a culture anchored in meaning and purpose.

PHASE 3 – EMPOWER		
There is a gap between leadership and managerial acumen to steward a workplace anchored in meaning and purpose that is equipped to address issues identified in the Purpose/Culture assessment and people process audit.	Vitally Inspired: Living and Leading Through Purpose™ program – to awaken leaders to their passion and purpose, and lead from inspiration. Managing Through Meaning™ program – teaches essential management practices and ways to create a work environment where employees can find meaning.	Inspiring leaders and managers of meaning are growing everywhere in the company, activating the growth, development, and contribution of all team members.
PHASE 4 – EMPLOY		
Leaders recognize the opportunity to enroll and align all stakeholders to the company's purpose, mission, and vision. Leaders recognize the need to cascade meaning and purpose across the full organization to make it "stick."	Parliament of Purpose Assembly – stakeholder session is facilitated to unite over and upgrade the company's purpose, mission, and vision. All team members enroll in Grab Your Gusto content to teach them to activate meaning and purpose in their everyday work.	Stakeholders emerge enlivened, united, and inspired to realize the company's purpose. The GYG content arouses and "lifts" everyone, fortifying a cultural transformation anchored in meaning and purpose.

As John Coleman[31] and I discussed on air,[32] and as I consult with organizations in their purpose journey, it's important to bear in mind the following when crafting and living your company purpose:

- Engage the organization comprehensively (discussed earlier): This means involving everyone in the company or department (or team, even) to work to articulate purpose. I like to call this the "wild, alive scratching" process where individuals and then the group struggle to say, exactly, just why the organization exists and why anyone should care. It's the scratching part that enrolls each individual on a visceral level, gains their buy-in, and connects to their limbic brain to make it meaningful.

- Periodically revisit your mission and values: As your company evolves with new leadership or team members, the mission of your purpose expressed through products and services can change to remain relevant to customers. Your values can and will likely evolve as the consciousness of your leaders and teams do as well.

- Recognize those who live the company's purpose and values: Showcasing and thanking individuals who "walk the talk" of your purpose is a great way to both illustrate what you believe to be ideal purpose expression while also teaching the rest of the organization what it looks like.

- Encourage both top-down and bottom-up approaches to purpose: It's good practice to consider how both your most senior leaders articulate your organization's purpose (because it may be closer to the original founder or previous leadership) and the view of those on the front lines (who may see it playing out differently or benefit from learning the original reason the organization was formed).

- Be flexible: This is where being able to adapt to a changing world while staying true to your original service intention can be extremely useful, especially in living your purpose.
- Listen at all levels of the organization: Just as you'll involve representatives from across the organization, if not all team members, it's critical all levels in the organization have a voice in the articulation of your purpose and that you hear and understand how they are living that purpose, for consistency and continuity.
- Communicate consistently: Speaking about your company purpose in a crisp, consistent way helps keep the heartbeat of purpose alive, nurturing the full organization.

Sisodia and Gelb say in the age of transcendence in which we are now living, people are looking for higher levels of meaning, not just what they own or consume – becoming the soul of capitalism. A defined and activated "why" that gets leaders and team members going above and beyond just coming to work and being paid can become a force for change in the organization and elsewhere. "When this why is defined, written down, and put into action throughout the organization, it exponentially enlarges its impact."[33]

Embed Your Company Purpose into Every Operational Aspect

Having read as far as you have, you have distinguished yourself from many other leaders who think of purpose functionally or instrumentally, regarding it as a tool they can wield. Just as your purpose evolves and deepens with your own consciousness, so does its expression and reach into your organization. Adopt the "Deep Purpose" leader mindset and think of purpose as something more fundamental: an *existential* statement that expresses your company's very reason for being and sets bold goals that clearly embrace commercial logic but go beyond to serve deeper moral values. Treat your company's purpose as an existential intention that informs every decision, practice, and process, the operating system that animates the life of your company.[34] In other words, embed deep purpose into your company's operations such that it serves as your North Star navigational system in everything you do.

The most effective and inspirational leaders embed this purpose in their organizations through operational practices *and* their well-honed communication skills as storytellers, something I wrote about in *Purpose Ignited*.[35] Become intentional about embedding purpose deeply into your everyday operations by sharing inspiring stories about customers and employees, which will open, soften, and humanize your organization. These stories you tell will showcase that your company is serving a purpose that transcends financial performance. "Compelling storytelling," defined in the broadest sense as the depiction of one or more events transpiring over time, helps people feel the purpose by letting them watch it come to life before their eyes![36] Fold into your practice of storytelling the discipline to go beyond specific, feel-good stories, to convey your company's purpose in a broader way that elevates your organization, convenes diverse stakeholders as a moral community, and sparks intense emotional bonds among you all. Your call to action is to learn to tell a grand, foundational story using rich, highly visual language about your company that lends depth, meaning, and even poetry to the enterprise. These stories "must evoke the company's values, trajectory, and destiny in a way that sticks with people and provides them with an enduring context in which to understand their daily operational realities."[37]

To become an effective storyteller, you will very likely need to improve your own communication skills. You can start by enrolling as a member in a local Toastmasters community,[38] as I did many years ago, to learn the basics of good speaking, build a foundation, and continue with other courses. I continue honing my speaking skills and have recently begun taking improv classes[39] to improve my ability to listen deeply, be fully present, be creative "on the fly," and add meaningfully to what my team members put forth in our mutual scene creations. Taking such classes does not mean you intend to be an actor or comedian, by the way, but can serve as fantastic professional development.

Embrace the "Deep Purpose" leadership mindset further by using it as a "sense-making" tool for action and continually evaluate your path forward. Orient your relationship to your company's purpose to influence the field of meaning and inform how your team members see and talk about decisions, products, processes, initiatives, and service to clients. Doing so will naturally generate a shared set of rules, conditions, assumptions, and emotions that govern your daily operations toward more value creation. Embrace the "both/and" mindset[40] (rather than either/or) to go beyond win-win solutions toward negotiating tradeoffs to arrive at the best possible solutions, staying ever nimble with your eyes riveted on your North Star of purpose. And this is critical – as you forge tradeoffs, robustly communicate them by explaining how these moves connect to and support your company's purpose. This requires explicit communication and will build necessary cohesion to stakeholders, especially when playing the long game as discussed in Chapter 1, by giving meaning to sacrifices you are making to achieve the goals and reinforce the field of meaning emanating from your company purpose.

Help Your Team Members Discover Their Own Purpose

The best and most productive way to activate "Deep Purpose" in your company is to elevate the care you show to individual employees, building on this theme discussed in Chapter 7. Develop your capacity to turn up your "spidey sense" to discern your people's uniqueness by acknowledging and engaging them as individuals to be celebrated. Encourage and support their development of the people they are striving to become, stepping further beyond encouraging the expression of their passion as discussed in Chapter 7, toward the fulfillment of their highest potential. Encourage and support your people to deepen their own self-understanding and explore their own purpose. To function on this level is to exist magnanimously and call forth their own highest and best self.

You can also align organizational purpose to team members' personal development and growth, which ignites intrinsic motivation and unleashes new levels of commitment and performance. As a Deep Purpose leader, work to craft humane and inclusive cultures that emphasize self-expression, growth, and individual purpose. Provide opportunities for individual employees to live the organizational purpose by connecting it with their own personal reasons for being.

If you want your team's full heart and soul, and to bring their "whole self" to work, they must first become aware of their own values, beliefs, and purpose in life. You also know from Chapter 4, Therapy, and Chapter 7, Open the Heart, that a strong and vital sense of self also includes constantly striving to reach one's potential and believing in one's ability to reach that potential. And it includes an alignment between one's purpose in life and the purpose in the work. As we'll also see, purpose yields a shared sense of identity, one rooted in belonging to a shared community.

It's essential for your employees to translate the corporate purpose into a personal work-related purpose of some kind. Doing so helps the purpose seem real to them, not just some meaningless formulation that corporate has dreamed up.

> When we talk about finding a calling, we're not just seeking an activity. We're looking for an identity, an understanding of who we are. We want to be complete, to make sense of the story of our lives. But whether we recognize it or not, this quest we've been talking about is not just a physical one; it's a spiritual one. It is, in a way, a journey of becoming.[41]

Louis Efron, a fellow purpose enthusiast and practitioner, sums up why helping your team members find and live their purpose helps your business as follows:

> People whose careers empower them to feel aligned with what they believe they have been put on Earth to do care more than those who aren't. These people feel a great sense of meaning, commitment, and pride in their work. This alignment is connected to the heart of what they do and who they are... They don't see their activities as work but as part of their lives. They would perform such duties without pay and frequently do on their own time or while trying to find paying work.[42]

Just as detecting and articulating company purpose is best stewarded with the help of a purpose guide, so is the journey to help your individual team members discover their own purpose. These are people's *lives* we're talking about here, so it's important to help them navigate their purpose journey with a competent professional. When you can help your team members discover this kind of depth in their own personal identity and purpose, you ignite a powerful and "sticky" connection with them. By sticky, I mean, they will want to remain with your organization because they feel a powerful bond to it. Then, when a recruiter calls with a new opportunity, they are less likely to investigate it or vacate their post, because they feel appreciation, gratitude, and connection to *you* for having helped them discover and engage themselves more deeply in their lives and work. You can offer various professional development workshops or courses to help them discover their strengths and values and even conduct them in-house with your own talent. When it comes to purpose exploration and discovery, bring in a subject matter expert in the field to help the team. Once your team members understand their own purpose, the next step is to help them see and thread their purpose and align it to that of your organization, as Nick Craig recommends.[43]

Elevate Your Company Purpose with Beauty

In your new capacity as a Deep Purpose leader, you have awakened in yourself and your team members an elevated creativity. You now more deeply recognize that business is far more than a profit machine, but rather "a vehicle for self-expression, for dreaming about and creating the future we desire, for accomplishing together what we cannot do alone, for creating extraordinary amounts of value of many kinds for everyone a business touches."[44] You learned in Chapter 1, Gumption, that you can architect your business model at a higher, more broadly serving level in a way that can breathe vital life into you the leader as well as all your stakeholders. It takes stepping back as well as gazing high and wide in your ecosystem of operations to accomplish, and it's wholly worth doing. Your ultimate job as a leader is:

> To bring brighter futures. Futures that… bring out the best in humanity. Create greater human value,

not just economic, political, or personal value. Bring about new possibilities, opportunities, equality, and freedom for more people. Burst with hope and feel better than we ever imagined possible.[45]

Once you've anchored your organization in its purpose, you can steward it into one that is "more impactful and exponentially more valuable."[46] As Morris says, consider this your invitational calling into a way of doing business, a way of playing the game of business with beauty, integrity, belonging, magnetism, and love at its core.[47]

Beauty is not the superficial adornment or the window dressing that the beauty industry would lead you to believe – it is a revolution of values that are inherited from the better angels of our nature. Beauty, in its truest and purest form, is a *felt sense* of the value system that sits in the marrow of your soul. It is who you are at your core. This is full-spectrum beauty.[48]

Said differently, "beauty" here is the fullest expression of your organization's purpose as lived in the world. Beauty is an aesthetic quality registered on Maslow's hierarchy of needs at one of the highest levels, and it aligns with increased consciousness. As our world continues to evolve to higher levels of consciousness and demands meaning and purpose across life, you win when you can provide what Morris calls "transcendent business experiences," which he explains in this passage:

Moreover, as our life and businesses increasingly become designed around the need to self-actualize, then self-transcend, Maslow reveals that we become more inclined to "peak experiences." The opportunity for peak experiences increases as a result of the biological, psychological, emotional, and spiritual development of individuals, cultures, and society at large. Maslow proposed that the difference between "nonpeakers" and "peakers" – that is, those who prefer status quo and those who welcome transformative experiences – is the separation of two groups of people: the explorers of the depths and heights, and those who bask in the comfort of being "tranquilized by the trivial."[49]

As you think on this matter, consider weaving into your operations the following principles offered by Morris to make yours a beautiful business:

- Put purpose to work
- Take agency of your evolution
- Activate self-awareness
- Cultivate trust and belonging
- Allow love to show up in your business
- Activate magnetism
- Live and work with soul
- Integrate your worlds
- Work with beauty.[50]

A beautiful business is a journey, a way of doing business, instigated by the leader's or leadership team's awakening to an evolved brand. To evolve toward a beautiful business, you need to understand the relationship between a business and a brand. Morris believes that the two are inseparable.[51]

Cultivating your own self-awareness over your life, leading authentically from your values, and aligning with your organization's purpose transforms you into an extremely compelling, inspirational leader. That kind of leadership is what allows you to create integrated teams aligned along the organization's purpose where people feel powerfully connected to those values which deepen the sense of belonging. And that combination ultimately builds trust and love. When teams are unified around a cause, they are ignited in their work, which together creates a magnetism.[52] There, then, is the beauty *and* ROI (return on investment) for building a beautiful business.

Expanding the beauty in your business model evolves over time. Consider your community of stakeholders and look for ways to extend your reach and impact as an organization into them. Stay anchored in your purpose as an organization and consider your values. To illustrate through example, let's say your organization operates in the Information Technology consulting industry. Listed among its values are: empowerment, sustainability, economic development, diversity. Here are some ideas to elevate beauty in this company's business model:

- Team members: In addition to a focus on recruiting new team members from diverse cultures, ages, and experiences, consider proactively reaching to historically disempowered groups such as veterans and neuro-diverse communities. Provide internships for foster kids to give them a path toward a career in IT.

- Customers: Can you reach to communities of people who need your service but wouldn't otherwise easily find you? Since your organization values economic development, perhaps you add a segment that provides IT services to under-performing schools in economically disadvantaged areas of your city? Doing so ultimately addresses economic development while elevating your impact and magnetizing others who similarly value such initiatives.

- Suppliers: Solicit vendors you wish to support to enable their success through your business together. Perhaps part of your strategy could include searching for IT sub-contractors from college students studying Computer Science.

- Investors: Look for collaborating investors who share your values and align on supporting your chosen employee or customer base.
- Community: Can you create a partnership or alliance with a non-profit organization in your community that supports providing IT training for families of foster children?

Beyond the organic approach shown above through example, a structured way you can add beauty to your company's purpose expression is to pursue B Corp certification, which proves the capacity to effectively balance purpose and profit. B Corp companies consider the impact of their operations on their employees, customers, suppliers, community, and the environment. Some well-known companies operating as B Corps include Danon USA, Patagonia, TOMS Shoes, and Katmandu. To become a B Corp requires you to undertake a B Impact Assessment and check your business operations against the pillars of governance, workers, community, environment, customer model.[53]

When we fuse forces in teams, cultures, and societies that are tapping into the higher angels of our nature, we can create exponential outcomes that even the best, brightest, and most powerful individuals cannot do on their own. This is what Brene Brown refers to as *collective effervescence.*[54]

Accept the Summons of Syntropy – Reaching to Our Higher Potential

This book opened with a promise to inform and lift your approach to leading your company to new heights by activating meaning and purpose. It finishes with a beacon call to expand your sights beyond your stakeholder ecosystem to the ecosystem at large. With what you have learned in this book, you are now positioned to "see" more of the world we live in than you could before, while recognizing its multitude of problems and dilemmas, with one being climate change. "Our situation is unprecedented: 'We are being pushed by Earth-sized ecological necessity and pulled by Universe-sized evolutionary opportunity.'"[55] Now you can begin to see the promise of a new frontier – living in a state of wholesome association with others on our planet through evolved principles and practices to scale human and planetary health by fostering a regenerative and abundant future.

This book has equipped you with an enlightened approach to leading your team and making a greater impact on your stakeholder community through your business. In part elevated through the world coming together in shared crisis during the pandemic, our single greatest collective need now is for what has been termed eco-awakening, "the somatic experience of being fully at home in the more-than-human world."[56] Gaze higher, reach higher, and you have a better shot at ascending in your leadership practice to channel your business for even greater good. There are so many problems in the world that desperately need to be addressed, and by operating your company through the best practices offered in Part 2 of this book, you simultaneously provide the nutritious meaning and purpose people crave. And yet, there's more.

Enter the "cosmosapien, a cosmic citizen, one who identifies with all points in space-time, whose understanding of self and purpose spans the vector of time – past, present, and future – and dimensions of space – height, width, and depth."[57] To know what it means to be us as humans, we must understand what it means to be connected to and in service of the cosmos as a whole. Titles and self-references frame identity and critically direct how we behave and communicate, and this term conveys so much in just 11 letters. It offers an identity and perspective that has been missing to various visions put forth to make the world a better place and more dynamically fulfill our lives in the process. Let us situate this elixir of possibility through a passage in Peele's book, *Planet on Purpose*:

> We are becoming, as cosmologist Brian Swimme has illuminated, the awakened Cosmos, simultaneously aware that we are aware (*sapiens sapiens*) and increasingly aware that what is aware is not just a human, but the Cosmos itself. We are now engaged in a giant intellectual and physical waking up process, a feline morning stretch across all dimensions of space-time (time-height-width-depth), getting oriented to our body (the Cosmos) and just now beginning to think about what to do with our careers and the Earth's political economy from this new awareness.[58]

As a cosmosapien, "we now stretch, awaken with our wisdom traditions, with purpose discovery work, dancing with art and science, faith and technology, mystery and reason, creating the synapses and muscle memory required to ambulate as this new identity, *Cosmosapien*."

> As the emerging central nervous systems of the Cosmos; and as the multi-perspectival beating heart of existence – we are now unified and empowered to achieve collectively what would otherwise be impossible. We now have a new planetary and species mythology, a code of conduct and declaration informed by science, a new reason to find and live our purpose individually, to be a stand for others to find their purpose and make their greatest contribution, to restore integrity, through the vehicle of purpose, to every unit of human cooperation and create a planet that works for every living being.[59]

When we direct ourselves to something or someone beyond ourselves – which allows us to self-actualize, a side effect of self-transcendence (as you learned about in Chapter 7 in the job purposing section), we become more tangibly aware of our implicit connection to and co-evolution of the cosmos.[60]

> At the individual level, over time we move towards more syntropy, or what the religious among us might call grace – the embodiment of wisdom and compassion or the nature and will of God. We experience this as a call towards living our own code structure, our purpose, our own conscious/psycho-spiritual core, toward biological health, and in cooperation with the collective code structure, the Cosmic purpose, towards greater economic and social prosperity, ecological diversity, creative self-expression, and social actualization. With a syntropic orientation, we yearn to be what we are at every level: living our purpose, exercising our powers, so that the next lines of human code can be written for the greatest benefit of all, reaching ever higher levels of integrity, beauty, and actualization, syntropy is not merely an individual human phenomenon, but a collective one as well.[61]

Breathtaking, isn't it? Dense and meaty, to be sure. To adopt a syntropy mindset and achieve cosmosapien status requires awakening "the latent meaning in our souls to ignite the broader purpose of transforming society into a more compassionate, ecological, and cooperative global community."[62] If this idea seems far-fetched or overly lofty, consider how the fields of meaning and purpose continue to evolve and mature. Gulati's direction of "deep purpose" shared in this book is fresh and takes purpose to an elevated state of operations seldom discussed in business circles. Paul Skinner's new book, released in late 2022, *The Purpose Upgrade: Change Your Business to Save the World – Change the World to Save Your Business*, discusses how businesses can repurpose and revitalize the activities they engage in through an enlightened perspective.[63] In stepping on the path to eco-awakening, you will be enchanted by the company you keep, the supportive community you gain, and the magnificence of your own unfoldment of your potential both as a leader and an organization. Open your mind, heart, and soul NOW.

Key Points Summary

❖ Do the work – be a leader worth following. Your own level of consciousness and corresponding development is the ceiling to the growth in your organization. Your work on yourself to improve your capacity to lead effectively is never complete.

❖ Add inspiration to evolve your leadership practice. Effective leadership in today's times is inspirational leadership. Your job as a leader is to communicate worth and potential in young people and lead them to their greatness.

❖ Detect your company's purpose – your unique way of being and serving. People want to be part of organizations they are proud of, and they will opt in to work with you when your company purpose is compelling for them. That takes fully detecting and articulating so it lives daily in their lives and inspires them to give their best efforts in service of that purpose.

❖ Help your team members discover their own purpose. People crave learning about their unique talents and what they believe they are here to do in fulfillment of their own purpose. Help them find that and align it with and through your company purpose, and your organization is *on fire*!

❖ Embed your company purpose into every operational aspect. Purpose is not a convenience label. Rather it should serve as the organizational heartbeat that governs all behavior and communication, woven deeply through your culture. Work purpose deeply into the organization so that you've embedded structure that is the purpose echo cascading its message through every action.

❖ Elevate the beauty in your business model. Your business is a powerful engine and can do even more good in the world when you seek new and creative ways to operate. Look for stakeholder sub-communities you can lift and in so doing further express your purpose.

❖ Accept the summons of syntropy – reaching to our higher potential. Step on the journey toward eco-awakening to develop your capacity to continue doing business that betters the world through enlightened inspirational leaders and seek sustainability on a healthy planet that works for all its inhabitants.

By reading this book, it's clear you're out to reach new heights of leading your company today and stewarding higher consciousness tomorrow. Take stock of your organization and identify your opportunities for improvement by completing the checklist below. Indicate your rating of each practice in your organization as follows:

1 – Never

2 – Rarely

3 – Sometimes

4 – Most of the Time

5 – Always

Elevated Practice	Description	1	2	3	4	5
Be a leader worth following	You have adopted the mantra of ongoing improvement and are actively working to cultivate your own self-awareness and self-development through reading, training, and/or coaching.					
Add inspiration to your leadership	You and your leadership team are active proponents of leading through communicating worth and potential to each team member and inspiring them through the vision you cast.					
Detect your company's purpose	Your company's purpose is fully articulated and understood by all team members.					
Help your team members discover their purpose	In service of helping your employees realize their best lives, you have invested in supporting their journey to discover their own purpose – and ideally, helped them align it with and through that of your company's purpose.					
Embed your company purpose into operations	You have thoroughly embedded your company purpose through all operations such that it informs your interactions and communications with all stakeholders and serves to orient choices and decisions across the whole enterprise.					

Elevate the beauty in your business	You have embedded additional layers of "beauty" in your company by seeking more ways to express your company purpose by more dynamically serving your stakeholders and thereby improving more people's lives.					
Accept the summons and reach for your higher potential	You are actively seeking enlightened ways of living and doing business by studying conscious leadership practices and stewarding eco-awakening and eco-connecting in your company.					

Conclusion

I am very glad our paths have crossed, thanks to you picking up this book. We live in dynamic times, and I'm convinced we all need to be consciously rowing our collective boats in the same direction – upstream.

This book is offered to you as one-part navigational system and one-part instructional inspiration. Through the GUSTO NOW orientation, you have been equipped to tap into your own gusto to keep yourself fortified as a leader and steward your organization toward its optimal health and well-being. You will continue to be tested as leader as the dynamics of the marketplace constantly change and evolve – all the more reason why keeping your G, gumption, square in your mind's eye will be a critical orientation. To achieve this requires vigilance, a focus on this centering prize.

Operating with U, urgency, compels you to pay attention to the trends that pull society and business forward and move with alacrity toward them. To live with this heightened sense of urgency implies being in a constant state of openness and agency. Vim, vigor, and verve all signal a firm sense of aliveness. This is what's required to remain relevant in today's times. Minding your S, sustainability, in all matters across life is not only a business imperative but a necessary move toward ongoing eco-awakening and a broadening of human consciousness. Just as we care for our individual selves through good diet and exercise, so must we care for the home that makes our living possible.

Meaning and purpose are vital sources of energy and are critical components of a fulfilled life. Your organization, and the way you lead it, are a bountiful treasure trove of these staples. You can activate meaning in your organization through the T of therapy – logotherapy to be more precise. Logotherapy is your constant source of instruction and aid that guides your behavior and communication to activate invaluable intrinsic motivation among your team members by helping them discover meaning in their everyday work. With this foundational premise established, you are then well positioned to leverage the power of O, Ownership through Purpose. When each person in your organization fully understands your company purpose and is on fire to realize your vision, that unified limbic resonance vitalizes engaged contribution and better informs decision-making to achieve it.

With GUSTO fortifying your own breath and that of your organization, you are now well positioned to apply the best practices of NOW to continue stewarding it to new heights. Applying the rational power of IQ through the N of Nurture, you will audit all processes and procedures that impact your people. You are looking for any obstacles that stint personal expression and creative contribution. Starting with your employment brand to attract the team you want, to the hiring and onboarding of new members, and on how you reward and promote, each process touching your people must be evaluated to humanize your workplace and encourage engagement, performance, and retention.

There is so much you can do to Open (O) the hearts of your people by elevating emotionally intelligent practices throughout your management team. Hiring caring managers and developing their capacity to manage through meaning in everyday matters is good for your own well-being and is veritable heart health for everyone. Teaching your managers to activate meaning in everyday interactions improves well-being by increasing vital connection and stoking invaluable intrinsic motivation that fuels performance and innovation. It turns out that addressing matters of the heart in the workplace is good for the bottom line. If you only addressed the practices of N and O to nurture mindfully your people practices and open the hearts of your people, you would be in a much better position to effectively operate in today's times. And yet, there's so much *more* to life and business. Learning to Wake (W) your soul and that of your team members incredibly fortifies your capacity to make a contribution through your company that truly betters the world. Articulating and declaring the soul, or purpose, of your company is vital to attract, enable, and keep today's workforce. They hunger for meaning and purpose, and your ability to operate through your purpose is the nutrition that sustains.

COVID-19 and increased consciousness about the associated climate crisis recently catalyzed our great, preexisting sense of urgency, and ushered in the imperative to elevate business. This movement has been driven by a coalition of employees, consumers, customers, investors, and the media, all scrutinizing every move business makes. When urgency met higher expectations, the ongoing change accelerated. So, the present and intermediate future requires more "proof of purpose" (POP) – the actions your company takes, your products or services as the embodiment of your values, and your ability to effectively communicate your impact. If you truly intend to build lasting trust-based relationships with your stakeholders and become part of the solution to our grave collection of coming disasters, you are well served to do so through a focus on bolstering your POP.[1] Adopting the identity of a cosmosapien working toward syntropy hurls you toward this status, with *GUSTO*. Raise your gaze, be bold, and reach for the stars.

Bibliography

Baird, J., & Sullivan, E. (2022). *Leading with Heart: Five Conversations that Unlock Creativity, Purpose, and Results.* HarperCollins Publishers.

Banks, K. (2022). *The Pursuit of Purpose: Part Memoir, Part Study – A Book About Finding Your Way in the World.* kiwanja.net.

Barnes, J. (2018). *Ikigai: Discover Your Reason for Being.* Sterling Ethos.

Barnes, J. (2020). *Sisu: Find Your Resilience the Finnish Way (the Nordic Way).* Sterling Ethos.

Beeny, C. (2020). *What's Your Shine? A Method for Discovering Who You Are and Why It Matters.* CKB Group, LLC.

Bhatnagar, G., & Minukas, M. (2022). *Unfear: Transform Your Organization to Create Breakthrough Performance and Employee Well-Being.* McGraw Hill.

Boccalandro, B. (2021). *Do Good at Work: How Simple Acts of Social Purpose Drive Success and Wellbeing.* Morgan James Publishing.

Bronson, P. (2005). *What Should I Do with My Life? The True Story of People Who Answered the Ultimate Question.* Ballantine Books.

Brown, S. (2020). *The Innovation Ultimatum: How Six Strategic Technologies Will Reshape Every Business in the 2020s.* John Wiley & Sons, Inc.

Bruner, J. (2002). *Making Stories: Law, Literature, Life.* Farrar, Straus and Giroux.

Buckingham, M., & Goodall, A. (2019). *Nine Lies About Work: A Freethinking Leader's Guide to the Real World.* Harvard Business Review Press.

Calderoni, F. A. (2021). *Upstanding: How Company Character Catalyzes Loyalty, Agility, and Hypergrowth.* John Wiley & Sons, Inc.

Catmull, E. (2014). *Creativity, Inc.: Overcoming the Unseen Forces that Stand in the Way of True Inspiration.* Bantam Press.

Chapman, B., & Sisodia, R. (2015). *Everybody Matters: The Extraordinary Power of Caring for Your People Like Family.* Portfolio Penguin.

Chen Nielsen, N., & Tillisch, N. (2021). *Return on Ambition: A Radical Approach to Your Achievement, Growth, and Well-Being.* Fast Press Company.

Ciaramicoli, A. P. (2021). *America Reunited: A Relational Solution to Bridging the Political, Social and Personal Chasm Dividing Our Nation.* Open Books.

Ciaramicoli, A. P., & Crystal, J. (2019). *The Soulful Leader: Success with Authenticity, Integrity and Empathy.* Open Books.

Clark, P. (2022). The Man Who Predicted the Great Resignation Says Quitting's Contagious. *Financial Review.* www.afr.com/work-and-careers/careers/the-man-who-predicted-the-great-resignation-says-quitting-s-contagious-20220406-p5abbc

Clifton, J., & Harter, J. (2021). *Wellbeing at Work: How to Build Resilient and Thriving Teams.* Gallup Press.

Cohen, D. (2017). *What Will They Say About You When You're Gone? Creating a Life of Legacy.* (2017).

Coleman, J. (2022). *HBR Guide to Crafting Your Purpose.* Harvard Business Review Press.

Comber, J. (2020). *The Forces of Collaborative Creativity: A Practical Guide to Creative Teamwork in the Healthcare Business.* Practical Inspiration Publishing.

Conscious Capitalism. www.consciouscapitalism.org/

Cortez, A. M. (2005). *Identity at Work: Modes of Engagement Among High-Performance Information Technology Managers* [dissertation, Fielding Graduate University]. Santa Barbara.

Cortez, A. (2020). *Purpose Ignited: How Inspiring Leaders Unleash Passion and Elevate Cause* [business, inspiration, leadership]. Practical Inspiration Publishing.

Cortez, A. (2020). Caring for Your Living Organization in *Working on Purpose.* R. Ciolino (October 14). www.voiceamerica.com/episode/126201/caring-for-your-living-organization

Cortez, A. (Ed.). (2021). *Passionately Striving in "Why": An Anthology of Women Who Persevere Mightily to Live Their Purpose.* Something or Other Publishing Inc.

Cortez, A. (2022). High Performance Companies Operate from Deep Purpose in *Working on Purpose*. W. C. Radio. www.iheart.com/podcast/209-working-on-purpose-28429595/episode/high-performance-companies-operate-from-deep-purpose-93008529/

Cortez, A. (2022). *Serving from "How" and "Why": Creating Workplaces, Led by Leaders Who Inspire Greatness, in Companies Doing Business That Better The World*. (Viktor Frankl Institute of Logotherapy). Abilene, TX.

Cortez, A. M., & Lynch, O. H. (2015). Zones of Engagement: Where Meaning in Work Meets Personal Identity. *International Journal of Human Resources Development and Management, 15*, nos. 2–4: 170–184.

Covey, S. R., & Covey Haller, C. (2022). *Live Life in Crescendo: Your Most Important Work is Always Ahead of You*. Simon & Schuster.

Craig, N. (2018). *Leading from Purpose: Clarity and the Confidence to Act When it Matters Most*. Hachette Books.

Cutting, D. (2022). *Employees First! Inspire, Engage, and Focus on the HEART of Your Organization*. Career Press.

Csikszentmihalyi, M. (1991). *Flow: The Psychology of Optimal Experience*. Harper Perennial.

DeKoster, L. (1982). *Work: The Meaning of Your Life*. Christian's Library Press, Inc.

Dik, B. J., Byrne, Z. S., & Steger, M. F. (Eds.). (2013). *Purpose and Meaning in the Workplace*. American Psychological Association.

Dillon. (2021). What is Stakeholder Capitalism and Why is it Dangerous? *Main Street Crypto*. https://mainstreetcrypto.com/articles/what-is-stakeholder-capitalism/

Duckworth, A. (2016). *Grit: The Power of Passion and Perseverance.* Scribner.

Dweck, C. S. (2006). *Mindset: The New Psychology of Success.* Ballantine Books.

Dyer, D. W. W. (2010). *The Shift: Taking Your Life from Ambition to Meaning.* Hay House, Inc.

Efron, L. (2017). *Purpose Meets Execution: How Winning Organizations Accelerate Engagement and Drive Profit.* Bibliomotion.

Elgin, D. (2017). Humanity's Journey Home: Learning to Live in a Living Universe. In E. Kuntzelman & D. DiPerna (Ed.), *Purpose Rising: A Global Movement of Transformation and Meaning* (pp. 129–150). Bright Alliance.

Erlich, P., & Reed, J. (dir.) (2020). *My Octopus Teacher.* Off the Fence, The Sea Change Project, Netflix.

Esfahani Smith, E. (2017). *The Power of Meaning: Finding Fulfillment in a World Obsessed with Happiness.* Broadway Books.

Fabry, J. B. (2013). *The Pursuit of Meaning: Viktor Frankl, Logotherapy, and Life.* Purpose Research, LLC.

Firth, J., & Zintz, A. (2020). *Grit, Grace & Gravitas: The Three Keys to Transforming Leadership, Presence, and Impact.* Open Door Publications.

Fischer, E. F. (2014). *The Good Life: Aspiration, Dignity, and the Anthropology of Wellbeing*. Stanford University Press.

Frankl, V. E. (1988). *The Will to Meaning: Foundations and Applications of Logotherapy*. Meridian.

Frankl, V. E. (2006). *Man's Search for Meaning*. Beacon Press.

Gallup. (2022). *Workplace*. www.gallup.com/workplace/229424/employee-engagement.aspx?msclkid=9228bc4e94691ab41127de38ec152392&utm_source=bing&utm_medium=cpc&utm_campaign=workplace_branded_employee_engagement&utm_term=gallup%20employee%20engagement&utm_content=Gallup%20Engagement%20%

Gallup. (2021). State of the Global Workplace 2021 Report. www.gallup.com/workplace/349484/state-of-the-global-workplace.aspx

Gamst, F. C. (Ed.). (1995). *Meanings of Work: Considerations for the Twenty-First Century*. State University of New York Press.

Garcia, H., & Miralles, F. (2019). *The Book of Ichigo Ichie: The Art of Making the Most of Every Moment, the Japanese Way*. Penguin Books.

Goins, J. (2015). *The Art of Work: A Proven Path to Discovering What You Were Meant to Do*. Nelson Books.

Graber, A. V. (2004). *Viktor Frankl's Logotherapy: Method of Choice in Ecumenical Pastoral Psychology* (2nd ed.). Wyndham Hall Press.

Graham, R. E. (1997). *50-50 at 50: Going Just Beyond*. Pacific Rim Publishers.

Gratton, L. (2022). *Redesigning Work: How to Transform Your Organization and Make Hybrid Work for Everyone*. The MIT Press.

Grayson, D., Coulter, C., & Lee, M. (2018). *All In: The Future of Business Leadership*. Routledge.

Gulati, R. (2022). *Deep Purpose: The Heart and Soul of High-Performance Companies*. HarperCollins Publishers.

Gustin, J. (2017). Discovering Purpose: Soulwork and the Purpose Octagon. In E. Kuntzelman & D. DiPerna (Ed.), *Purpose Rising: A Global Movement of Transformation and Meaning* (pp. 39–72). Bright Alliance.

Gutknecht, D., & Lahey, S. (2017). *Meaning at Work and Its Hidden Language*. Aviri Publishing.

Haden, J. (2018). *The Motivation Myth: How High Achievers Really Set Themselves Up to Win*. Portfolio Penguin.

Hall, D., Feldman, E., & Kim, N. (2013). Meaning Work and the Protean Career. In B. J. Dik, Z. S. Byrne, & M. F. Steger (Ed.), *Purpose and Meaning in the Workplace* (pp. 57–68). American Psychological Association.

Hare, A. (2020). *Lead Brighter by Navigating Through the Unfolding Path*. Tournesol.

Harini, Y. N. (2015). *Sapiens: A Brief History of Humankind*. Harper Perennial.

Henry, T. (2013). *Die Empty: Unleash Your Best Work Every Day*. Portfolio Penguin.

Hollis, J. (2006). *Finding Meaning in the Second Half of Life: How to Finally, Really Grow Up*. Gotham Book.

Hoyos, K. (2019). *Purpose: The Ultimate Quest.* Post Hill Press.

Hulsey, T. (2018). *The Winning Mindset that Saved My Life.* Lovett Press International.

Hurst, A. (2014). *The Purpose Economy: How Your Desire for Impact, Personal Growth and Community is Changing the World.* Elevate.

Iloenyosi, K. (2012). *Finding Your Sweet Spot: Where Your Talents, Interests and Passions Converge to Deliver the Life You Were Born to Live.* BookLogix.

Iloenyosi, K. (2016). *DNA of Talent: A Blueprint for Discovering Your Talents and Putting Them to Work.* BookLogix.

Janse, D., & Bogers, M. (2020). *Getting Started with Holacracy: Upgrading Your Team's Performance.* Diederick Janse and Marco Bogers.

Johnson, M. (2019). Intrinsic Motivation: The Drive Beyond Employee Engagement in *Working on Purpose.* R. Ciolino (May 28). www.voiceamerica.com/episode/115372/intrinsic-motivation-the-drive-beyond-employee-engagement

Kaufman, S. B. (2020). *Transcend: The New Science of Self-Actualization.* TarcherPerigree.

Kegan, R., & Lahey, L. L. (2016). *An Everyone Culture: Becoming a Deliberately Developmental Organization.* Harvard University Press.

Kimble, M. A., & Ellor, J. W. (2001). Logotherapy: An Overview. In M. A. Kimble (Ed.), *Viktor Frankl's Contribution to Spirituality and Aging* (pp. 9–24). Routledge.

Kromme, C. (2017). *Humanifiation Go Digital, Stay Human: How Technology Will Advance Humanity Towards a More Meaningful Future.* The Choir Press.

Kuntzelman, E., & DiPerna, D. (Ed.). (2017). *Purpose Rising: A Global Movement of Transformation and Meaning* (1st ed.). Bright Alliance.

Kurtz, E., & Ketcham, K. (1992). *The Spirituality of Imperfection: Storytelling and the Search for Meaning.* Bantam Books.

Laszlo, E. (2017). In Search of the Purpose of Being: Cosmic Insights for Enduring Human Life on the Planet. In E. Kuntzelman & D. DiPerna (Ed.), *Purpose Rising: A Global Movement of Transformation and Meaning* (pp. 29–38). Bright Alliance.

Linley, P. A. (2013). Human Strengths and Well-Being: Finding the Best Within Us at the Intersection of Eudaimonic Philosophy, Humanistic Psychology, and Positive Psychology. In A. S. Waterman (Ed.), *The Best Within Us: Positive Psychology Perspectives on Eudaimonia* (pp. 269–286). American Psychological Association.

Lukas, E. (2015). *The Therapist and the Soul: From Fate to Freedom.* Purpose Research, LLC.

Mainwaring, S. (2021). *Lead with WE: The Business Revolution that Will Save Our Future.* Matt Holt Books.

Martin, D. (2015). *Future Dreaming.* Documentary. www.davidmartin.world/future-dreaming

Mattiske, C. (2020). *Leading Virtual Teams: Managing From a Distance During the Coronavirus.* The Performance Company.

Maurer, R. (2021). Turnover "Tsunami" Expected Once Pandemic Ends. *Society for Human Resource Management*. www.shrm.org/resourcesandtools/hr-topics/talent-acquisition/pages/turnover-tsunami-expected-once-pandemic-ends.aspx

Mayer, K. (2021). What's Behind the Great Resignation? Blame Burnout. *Human Resource Executive*. https://hrexecutive.com/whats-behind-the-great-resignation-blame-burnout/

McDonald, K. (2021). *It's Time to Talk about Race at Work: Every Leader's Guide to Making Progress on Diversity, Equity, and Inclusion.* John Wiley & Sons, Inc.

Mercurio, Z. (2017). *The Invisible Leader: Transform Your Life, Work, and Organization with the Power of Authentic Purpose.* Advantage.

Milano, G. V. (2020). *Curing Corporate Short-Termism: Future Growth vs Current Earnings.* Fortuna Advisors.

Miller, A. (2022). A&M Professor Who Predicted "Great Resignation" Explains Potential Factors of Why Theory Came True. *The Eagle* (January 8). https://theeagle.com/news/a_m/a-m-professor-who-predicted-great-resignation-explains-potential-factors-of-why-theory-came-true/article_e99bb37c-6f29-11ec-9a2e-030d1c45b621.html#:~:text=The%20%E2%80%9CGreat%20Resignation%E2%80%9D%E2%80%94%20coined%20and%20

Mitchell, M. H. (2017). *Kinetic Life: Unleash Your Potential.* Drive Influence LLC.

Monger, K. (2017). *Common Sense Transition: A Call to Action and a Blueprint for Change.* Creative Team Publishing.

Morris, S. (2021). *The Beautiful Business: An Actionable Manifesto to Create an Unignorable Business with Love at the Core.* Conscious Capitalism Press.

Palmer, P. J. (2000). *Let Your Life Speak: Listening for the Voice of Vocation.* Jossey-Bass.

Pattakos, A., & Dundon, E. (2015). *The OPA! Way: Finding Joy & Meaning in Everyday Life & Work.* BenBella Books, Inc.

Pattakos, A., & Dundon, E. (2017). *Prisoners of Our Thoughts: Viktor Frankl's Principles for Discovering Meaning in Life and Work.* Berrett-Koehler Publishers, Inc.

Patten, T. (2017). Integral Soul Work: Personal and Global Purpose. In E. Kuntzelman & D. DiPerna (Ed.), *Purpose Rising: A Global Movement of Transformation and Meaning* (pp. 151–162). Bright Allliance.

Peele, B. (2017). Your Purpose Expedition. In E. Kuntzelman & D. DiPerna (Ed.), *Purpose Rising: A Global Movement of Transformation and Meaning* (pp. 277–290). Bright Alliance.

Peele, B. (2018). *Planet on Purpose: Your Guide to Genuine Prosperity, Authentic Leadership and a Better World.* Balboa Press.

Plotkin, B. (2017). The Realm of Purpose Least Realized: But Most Essential in Our Time of Radical, Global Change. In E. Kuntzelman & D. DiPerna (Ed.), *Purpose Rising: A Global Movement of Transformation and Meaning* (pp. 73–102). Bright Alliance.

Plotkin, B. (2021). *The Journey of Soul Initiation: A Field Guide for Visionaries, Evolutionaries, and Revolutionaries.* New World Library.

Pursche, O. (2016). Investor Tip: Look for Purpose-Driven Companies. *Forbes.* www.forbes.com/sites/advisor/2016/07/06/investor-tip-look-for-purpose-driven-companies/?sh=1f0cbb383d6d

Ratoff, P. (2015). *Thriving in a Stakeholder World: Purpose as the New Competitive Advantage.* Indie Books International.

Robinson, K. (2011). *Out of Minds: Learning to be Creative.* Capstone Publishing.

Roth, B. (2018). *Strength in Stillness: The Power of Transcendental Meditation.* Simon & Schuster.

Ryan, R. M. C., Randall, R., & Deci, E. L. (2013). What Humans Need: Flourishing in Aristotelian Philosophy and Self-Determination Theory. In A. S. Waterman (Ed.), *The Best Within Us: Positive Psychology Perspectives on Eudaimonia* (pp. 57–76). American Psychological Association.

Scheler, M. (2009). *The Human Place in the Cosmos.* Northwestern University Press.

Seligman, M. E. P. (2011). *Flourish: A Visionary New Understanding of Happiness and Well-Being.* Atria Paperback.

Seneca Jankel, N. (2017). Purpose: The Bridge Between Consciousness and What Really Matters. In E. Kuntzelman & D. DiPerna (Ed.), *Purpose Rising: A Global Movement of Transformation and Meaning* (pp. 217–238). Bright Alliance.

Senge, P., Scharmer, C. O., Jaworski, J., & Flowers, B. S. (2004). *Presence: Human Purpose and the Field of the Future.* Crown Business.

Shore, H. M. (2020). *The Leader Launchpad: Five Steps to Fuel Your Business and Lift Your Profits*. Amplify Publishing.

Sinek, S. (2009). *Start with Why: How Great Leaders Inspire Everyone to Take Action*. Portfolio Penguin.

Sisodia, R., & Gelb, M. J. (2019). *The HEALING Organization: Awakening the Conscience of Business to Help Save the World*. HarperCollins Leadership.

Sisodia, R., Sheth, J., & Wolfe, D. B. (2014). *Firms of Endearment: How World-Class Companies Profit from Passion and Purpose* (2nd ed.). Pearson FT Press.

Skinner, P. (2018). *Collaborative Advantage: How Collaboration Beats Competition as a Strategy for Success*. Robinson.

Skinner, P. (2022). *The Purpose Upgrade: Change Your Business to Save the World. Change the World to Save Your Business*. Robinson.

Smith, W. K., & Lewis, M. W. (2022). *Both/And Thinking: Embracing Creative Tensions to Solve Your Toughest Problems*. Harvard Business Review Press.

Spiker, T. (2020). *The Only Leaders Worth Following: Why Some Leaders Succeed, Others Fail, and How the Quality of Our Lives Hangs in the Balance*. The Aperio Press.

Spodek, J. (2019). *Initiative: A Proven Method to Bring Your Passions to Life and Work*. Greenwich Lane Books.

Steinkruger, R. (2022). *Inspiration Universal and Unlimited: Motivation Scatters, Inspiration Gathers*. Stone Siel Press.

Stewart, R. M. (2019). *Unqualified Success: Bridging the Gap Between Where You Are Now and Where You Want to be to Achieve Massive Success*. Independent Publisher.

Stone Zander, R., & Zander, B. (2000). *The Art of Possibility: Transforming Professional and Personal Life*. Penguin Books.

Strecher, V. J. (2016). *Life on Purpose: How Living for what Matters Most Changes Everything*. HarperOne.

Swimme, B. T., & Tucker, M. E. (2011). *Journey of the Universe*. Yale University Press.

Syed, M. (2015). *Black Box Thinking: Marginal Gains and the Secrets of High Performance*. John Murray Publishers.

Thiyagarajan, S. (2017). *Born Wild: Journeys into the Wild Hearts of India and Africa*. Bloomsbury Publishing.

Thomson, J. (2021). The Great Resignation: COVID revealed how abnormal the modern workplace is. *Big Think*. https://bigthink.com/culture-religion/great-resignation-abnormal-modern-workplace

Tolle, E. (2005). *A New Earth: Awakening to Your Life's Purpose*. Penguin Group.

Warrick, S. (2021). *Tolerance and Diversity for White Guys and Other Human Beings: Living the Five Skills of Tolerance*. Ignite Press.

Westphal, D. (2021). *Convergence: Technology, Business, and the Human-Centric Future*. The Unnamed Press.

Winfrey, O. (2019). *The Path Made Clear: Discovering Your Life's Direction and Purpose*. Flatiron Book 5.

Wolfe, N. (2011). *The Living Organization: Transforming Business to Create Extraordinary Results*. Quantum Leaders Publishing.

Woods, H. (2020). *The Golden Thread: Where to Find Purpose in the Stages of Your Life*. New Degree Press.

Endnotes

Introduction

[1] Calderoni, *Upstanding* (2021).
[2] Ciaramicoli, *America Reunited* (2021).
[3] *Working on Purpose*, episode 392, iHeart Radio, The Workforce Rules Post COVID, August 4, 2022.
[4] *Working on Purpose*, episode 368, Voice America, High-Performance Companies Operate from Deep Purpose, February 23, 2022.
[5] Thomson, "The Great Resignation" (2021).
[6] Gallup, "Workplace" (2022).
[7] I find it delightful and enlightening that "meaning" translates to *significado* in both Spanish and Portuguese, as it connotes that which registers as significant to someone.
[8] Note that purpose translates in both Spanish and Portuguese to *propósito*.
[9] This definition is from Mercurio, *The Invisible Leader* (2017).
[10] You will learn about the principles of a "beautiful business" throughout this book, which draws on reading from and hosting the author of this book: Morris, *The Beautiful Business* (2021).

Part 1

[1] "Business Roundtable Redefines the Purpose of a Corporation to Promote 'An Economy That Serves All Americans,'" August 19, 2019, www.businessroundtable.org/business-roundtable-redefines-the-purpose-of-a-corporation-to-promote-an-economy-that-serves-all-americans
[2] Mainwaring, *Lead with WE* (2021).

Chapter 1

[1] Wolfe, *The Living Organization* (2011).
[2] Wolfe, *The Living Organization* (2011), p. 62.

[3] Westphal, *Convergence* (2021).

[4] Hare, *Lead Brighter* (2020), p. 46.

[5] *Working on Purpose*, episode 265, Voice America, Unleashing Business as the Force for Healing, March 4, 2020.

[6] www.consciouscapitalism.org

[7] Sisodia & Gelb, *The HEALING Organization* (2019), p. 20.

[8] Ratoff, *Thriving in a Stakeholder World* (2015).

[9] "Business Roundtable Redefines the Purpose of a Corporation to Promote 'An Economy That Serves All Americans,'" August 19, 2019, www.businessroundtable.org/business-roundtable-redefines-the-purpose-of-a-corporation-to-promote-an-economy-that-serves-all-americans

[10] Dillon, "What is Stakeholder Capitalism and Why is it Dangerous?" (2021).

[11] "Business Roundtable Redefines the Purpose of a Corporation to Promote 'An Economy That Serves All Americans,'" August 19, 2019, www.businessroundtable.org/business-roundtable-redefines-the-purpose-of-a-corporation-to-promote-an-economy-that-serves-all-americans

[12] Ratoff, *Thriving in a Stakeholder World* (2015).

[13] Sisodia et al., *Firms of Endearment* (2014).

[14] Sisodia et al., *Firms of Endearment* (2014).

[15] Sisodia et al., *Firms of Endearment* (2014).

[16] *Working on Purpose*, Voice America, episode 359, Profitable and Beautiful: Elevating Business to Soulful Heights, December 22, 2021.

[17] Morris, *The Beautiful Business* (2021), p. 20.

[18] Morris, *The Beautiful Business* (2021), p. 23.

[19] *Working on Purpose*, episode 359, Voice America, Profitable and Beautiful: Elevating Business to Soulful Heights, December 22, 2021.

[20] Morris, *The Beautiful Business* (2021), p. 33.

[21] Gulati, *Deep Purpose* (2022), p. xx.

[22] Milano, *Curing Corporate Short-Termism* (2020). Discussed in *Working on Purpose*, episode 360, Voice America, Short-Termism Be Gone: Investments for Total Shareholder Returns, December 29, 2021.

[23] Milano, *Curing Corporate Short-Termism* (2020).

[24] Milano, *Curing Corporate Short-Termism* (2020).

[25] Milano, *Curing Corporate Short-Termism* (2020), p. 8.

[26] Milano, *Curing Corporate Short-Termism* (2020), p. 11.

27 Westphal, *Convergence* (2021).

28 Milano, *Curing Corporate Short-Termism* (2020).

29 Milano, *Curing Corporate Short-Termism* (2020), p. 334.

Chapter 2

1 Learn more about Dr. Sangwan here: https://doctorneha.com

2 *Working on Purpose*, episode 344, Voice America, Business Leadership for a Human-Centric Future, September 8, 2021.

3 Westphal, *Convergence* (2021), p. 23.

4 Westphal, *Convergence* (2021), p. 103.

5 Westphal, *Convergence* (2021).

6 Westphal, *Convergence* (2021), p. 106.

7 Miller, "A&M Professor Who Predicted 'Great Resignation'" (January 8, 2022).

8 Clark, "The Man Who Predicted the Great Resignation" (2022).

9 Buckingham & Goodall, *Nine Lies About Work* (2019).

10 Seligman, *Flourish* (2011).

11 *Working on Purpose*, episode 315, Voice America, The Science of Purpose, Its Expression Potentials, and Our Cosmos, February 17, 2021.

12 Peele, *Planet on Purpose* (2018), p. 203.

13 Miller, "A&M Professor Who Predicted 'Great Resignation'" (January 8, 2022).

14 Cortez, *Purpose Ignited* (2020).

15 *Working on Purpose*, episode 368, Voice America, High-Performance Companies Operate from Deep Purpose, February 23, 2022.

16 Gratton, *Redesigning Work* (2022).

17 A reference to philosopher John Rawls' quip in the 1970s, as taken from Gratton, *Redesigning Work* (2022).

18 Cutting, *Employees First!* (2022).

19 Mayer, "What's Behind the Great Resignation?" (2021).

20 Clifton & Harter, *Wellbeing at Work* (2021).

21 Gratton, *Redesigning Work* (2022).

22 *Working on Purpose*, episode 278, Voice America, How Purpose Can Positively Impact the Mental Health Crisis, June 3, 2020.

23 Cutting, *Employees First!* (2022).

24 Gratton, *Redesigning Work* (2022).

[25] Mattiske, *Leading Virtual Teams* (2020).

[26] Mattiske, *Leading Virtual Teams* (2020).

[27] See https://urbanland.uli.org/economy-markets-trends/return-to-office-or-return-to-experience-top-execs-weigh-in/?utm_source=realmagnet&utm_medium=email&utm_campaign=HQ%20Urban%20Land%203%2E21%2E2022%20ab

[28] Mattiske, *Leading Virtual Teams* (2020).

Chapter 3

[1] Simply Insurance, *Average US Life Expectancy Statistics by Gender, Ethnicity & State* (2022). www.simplyinsurance.com/average-us-life-expectancy-statistics

[2] Grayson, Coulter, & Lee, *All In* (2018), p. 2.

[3] Grayson, Coulter, & Lee, *All In* (2018).

[4] For a wonderful deep dive into the history of humankind, check out Harini, *Sapiens* (2015).

[5] Elgin, "Humanity's Journey Home" (2017), p. 147.

[6] Foster & Thiyagarajan, *My Octopus Teacher* (2020); Swimme & Tucker, *Journey of the Universe* (2011); Tolle, *A New Earth* (2005); Peele, *Planet on Purpose* (2018).

[7] Peele, *Planet on Purpose* (2018).

[8] Plotkin, "The Realm of Purpose Least Realized" (2017).

[9] Foster & Thiyagarajan, *My Octopus Teacher* (2020).

[10] Thiyagarajan, *Born Wild* (2017).

[11] Thiyagarajan, *Born Wild* (2017), p. 209.

[12] Scheler, *Human Place* (2009).

[13] Wolfe, *The Living Organization* (2011).

[14] Wolfe, *The Living Organization* (2011).

[15] Brown, *The Innovation Ultimatum* (2020); Sisodia et al., *Firms of Endearment* (2014).

[16] Ratoff, *Thriving in a Stakeholder World* (2015); Sisodia & Gelb, *The HEALING Organization* (2019).

[17] Grayson, Coulter, & Lee, *All In* (2018), p. 2.

[18] Grayson, Coulter, & Lee, *All In* (2018), p. 4.

[19] Grayson, Coulter, & Lee, *All In* (2018).

[20] Grayson, Coulter, & Lee, *All In* (2018), p. 5.

[21] Mainwaring, *Lead with WE* (2021), p. 52.

[22] Westphal, *Convergence* (2021).

23 Elgin, "Humanity's Journey Home" (2017), p. 130.
24 Elgin, "Humanity's Journey Home" (2017), p. 130.
25 Elgin, "Humanity's Journey Home" (2017), p. 131.
26 Elgin, "Humanity's Journey Home" (2017), p. 140.
27 Elgin, "Humanity's Journey Home" (2017), p. 143.
28 Elgin, "Humanity's Journey Home" (2017), p. 144.
29 *Beyond Zero*, directed by N. Havey, released 2020.
30 Mainwaring, *Lead with WE* (2021), p. 13.
31 U.S. Securities and Exchange Commission, *SEC Proposes Rules to Enhance and Standardize Climate-Related Disclosures for Investors* (2022). www.sec.gov/news/press-release/2022-46
32 Westphal, *Convergence* (2021).
33 Gulati, *Deep Purpose* (2022).
34 Gulati, *Deep Purpose* (2022).
35 Calderoni, *Upstanding* (2021).
36 Calderoni, *Upstanding* (2021).
37 Calderoni, *Upstanding* (2021), pp. 19–20.
38 Calderoni, *Upstanding* (2021).
39 Grayson, Coulter, & Lee, *All In* (2018).
40 Calderoni, *Upstanding* (2021), p. 66.
41 Calderoni, *Upstanding* (2021), p. 119.
42 Calderoni, *Upstanding* (2021), p. 121.

Chapter 4

1 Esfahani Smith, *The Power of Meaning* (2017).
2 Esfahani Smith, *The Power of Meaning* (2017), p. 5.
3 Cortez, *Purpose Ignited* (2020).
4 Frankl, *The Will to Meaning* (1988).
5 Gutknecht & Lahey, *Meaning at Work* (2017), p. 67.
6 Visit the Viktor Frankl Institute of America website for more information at: https://viktorfranklamerica.com/what-is-logotherapy
7 Frankl, *Man's Search for Meaning* (2006).
8 Visit this website for more information about courses and certification: www.viktorfranklinstitute.org
9 Cortez, *Serving from "How" and "Why"* (2022).
10 Pattakos & Dundon, *The OPA! Way* (2015); Pattakos & Dundon, *Prisoners of Our Thoughts* (2017).
11 Visit for more information: www.globalmeaninginstitute.com

12 Kimble & Ellor, "Logotherapy" (2001), p. 9.

13 Frankl, *The Will to Meaning* (1988).

14 Frankl, *Man's Search for Meaning* (2006).

15 Cortez, *Purpose Ignited* (2020).

16 Fabry, *Pursuit of Meaning* (2013), pp. xix–xx.

17 Graber, *Viktor Frankl's Logotherapy* (2004).

18 Kimble & Ellor, "Logotherapy" (2001), p. 14.

19 Fabry, *Pursuit of Meaning* (2013).

20 Frankl, *Man's Search for Meaning* (2006); the goal of logotherapy is to stimulate the will to meaning, which is precisely how organizations can apply logotherapeutic principles by using them to inform cultural and leadership practices. Logotherapy focuses on meanings yet to be fulfilled and thus is meaning-centered psychotherapy.

21 Frankl, *The Will to Meaning* (1988), p.85.

22 Monger, *Common Sense Transition* (2017).

23 Pratt, Pradies, & Lepisto, in Dik, Byrne, & Steger, *Purpose and Meaning in the Workplace* (2013), p. 173.

24 The Manage Through Meaning program I created is designed to accomplish this very outcome.

25 See Hurst, *The Purpose Economy* (2014).

26 Pattakos & Dundon, *The OPA! Way* (2015).

27 Pattakos & Dundon, *The OPA! Way* (2015).

28 Craig, *Leading from Purpose* (2018).

29 Gutknecht & Lahey, *Meaning at Work* (2017), p. 60.

30 Gutknecht & Lahey, *Meaning at Work* (2017), p. 44.

31 Gutknecht & Lahey, *Meaning at Work* (2017), p. 45.

32 Gulati, *Deep Purpose* (2022), pp. 65–66.

33 Pattakos & Dundon, *The OPA! Way* (2015).

34 Lukas, *The Therapist and the Soul* (2015), p. 130.

Chapter 5

1 Wolfe, *The Living Organization* (2011), p. 2.

2 Cohen, *What Will They Say About You When You're Gone?* (2017), p. 118.

3 Mercurio, *The Invisible Leader* (2017).

4 Hare, *Lead Brighter* (2020), pp. 64–65.

5 Kuntzelman & DiPerna, *Purpose Rising* (2017).

[6] Hurst, *The Purpose Economy* (2014).

[7] Hurst, *The Purpose Economy* (2014).

[8] Strecher, *Life on Purpose* (2016).

[9] Hurst, *The Purpose Economy* (2014).

[10] Peele, *Planet on Purpose* (2018).

[11] Woods, *The Golden Thread* (2020).

[12] Cortez, *Passionately Striving in "Why"* (2021).

[13] Gulati, *Deep Purpose* (2022), p. 1.

[14] Shore, *The Leader Launchpad* (2020).

[15] Hurst, *The Purpose Economy* (2014), p. 3.

[16] Hurst, *The Purpose Economy* (2014), p. 24.

[17] Hurst, *The Purpose Economy* (2014).

[18] Wolfe, *The Living Organization* (2011).

[19] Gulati, *Deep Purpose* (2022), p. 2.

[20] Efron, *Purpose Meets Execution* (2017).

[21] Hurst, *The Purpose Economy* (2014).

[22] *Working on Purpose,* episode 191, Voice America, Aaron Hurst on the Purpose Economy, October 3, 2018.

[23] Hurst, *The Purpose Economy* (2014), p. 21.

[24] Hurst, *The Purpose Economy* (2014).

[25] Hoyos, *Purpose* (2019).

[26] Gulati, *Deep Purpose* (2022).

[27] *Working on Purpose,* episode 336, Voice America, July 14, 2021 and *Working on Purpose* Radio, You Tube, B Corps: Business as a Force for Profit and Purpose, streamed July 6, 2021.

[28] Shore, *The Leader Launchpad* (2020).

[29] Shore, *The Leader Launchpad* (2020), p. 255.

[30] Gulati, *Deep Purpose* (2022).

[31] Morris, *The Beautiful Business* (2021), pp. 234–235.

[32] Milano, *Curing Corporate Short-Termism* (2020).

[33] Milano, *Curing Corporate Short-Termism* (2020), p. 284.

[34] Mercurio, *The Invisible Leader* (2017).

[35] Visit www.dianemcclay.com to learn more about Diane McClay.

[36] Westphal, *Convergence* (2021).

[37] Gulati, *Deep Purpose* (2022).

[38] Gulati, *Deep Purpose* (2022), p. 54 paraphrased.

[39] Efron, *Purpose Meets Execution* (2017), p. 7.

[40] Efron, *Purpose Meets Execution* (2017).

[41] *Working on Purpose,* episode 269, Voice America, Thriving in Business: When Purpose Meets Execution, April 1, 2020.

[42] Shore, *The Leader Launchpad* (2020).

[43] *Working on Purpose,* episode 304, Voice America, Activating Purpose Through the Life Stages, December 2, 2020 and *Working on Purpose,* You Tube, Putting Purpose to Work Across the Life Stages, streamed November 24, 2020.

[44] Morris, *The Beautiful Business* (2021).

[45] *Working on Purpose,* Voice America, episode 335, Purpose and Profit: Today's Business Imperative, July 7, 2021.

[46] Pursche, "Investor Tip" (2016).

Part 2

[1] https://resurgenceblog.wordpress.com/2012/10/15/spiritual-intelligence-sq-better-work-better-life-better-being

[2] https://blog.mindvalley.com/iq-stands-for

[3] www.emotionalintelligencecourse.com/history-of-eq

[4] https://sqi.co/definition-of-spiritual-intelligence

[5] https://resurgenceblog.wordpress.com/2012/10/15/spiritual-intelligence-sq-better-work-better-life-better-being

[6] https://resurgenceblog.wordpress.com/2012/10/15/spiritual-intelligence-sq-better-work-better-life-better-being

Chapter 6

[1] Westphal, *Convergence* (2021).

[2] Kegan & Lahey, *An Everyone Culture* (2016).

[3] Gallup, *Workplace* (2022).

[4] Buckingham & Goodall, *Nine Lies About Work* (2019).

[5] From 2006 to 2010, I co-founded and co-led Improved Experience, an HR analytics tool that examined the hiring process experience and leverage the knowledge gained doing so in my consulting today.

[6] Steinkruger, *Inspiration Universal and Unlimited* (2022).

[7] To learn more about holacracy, listen to or watch *Working on Purpose,* episode 326, Voice America, May 5, 2021 or *Working on Purpose* Radio, Elevating Your Team's Performance with Holacracy,

You Tube, April 27, 2021 with co-author Marco Bogers and/or read their book: Janse & Bogers, *Getting Started with Holacracy* (2020).

[8] Start by reading this book: Milano, *Curing Corporate Short-Termism* (2020).

[9] Buckingham & Goodall, *Nine Lies About Work* (2019), p. 81.

[10] Buckingham & Goodall, *Nine Lies About Work* (2019), p. 94.

[11] *Working on Purpose*, episode 294, Voice America, September 20, 2020.

[12] Chapman & Sisodia, *Everybody Matters* (2015).

[13] Steinkruger, *Inspiration Universal and Unlimited* (2022), pp. 179–180.

[14] Buckingham & Goodall, *Nine Lies About Work* (2019).

[15] Mercurio, *The Invisible Leader* (2017).

[16] *Working on Purpose*, episode 310, January 13, 2021.

[17] Found on Goodreads.com, quote 5934.

[18] DeKoster, *Work* (1982); Dik, Byrne, & Steger, *Purpose and Meaning in the Workplace* (2013); Gamst, *Meanings of Work* (1995); Hall, Feldman, & Kim, "Meaning Work and the Protean Career" (2013).

[19] *Working on Purpose*, episode 368, Voice America, February 23, 2022.

[20] *Working on Purpose*, episode 395, Creating Compelling Workplaces that Attract Today's Discerning Talent, YouTube, August 23, 2022.

[21] Mattiske, *Leading Virtual Teams* (2020), p. 27.

[22] Mattiske, *Leading Virtual Teams* (2020), p. 30.

[23] Mattiske, *Leading Virtual Teams* (2020), p. 3.

[24] Mattiske, *Leading Virtual Teams* (2020), p. 42.

[25] Brown, *The Innovation Ultimatum* (2020), p. 66.

[26] Brown, *The Innovation Ultimatum* (2020), p. 158.

[27] Calderoni, *Upstanding* (2021).

[28] Brown, *The Innovation Ultimatum* (2020).

[29] *Working on Purpose*, episode 386, Connecting Remote Teams Through Virtual Experiences, Voice America, January 12, 22.

[30] Westphal, *Convergence* (2021), p. 111.

Chapter 7

[1] Firth & Zintz, *Grit, Grace & Gravitas* (2020).

[2] Chapman & Sisodia, *Everybody Matters* (2015), pp. 207–208.

[3] *Working on Purpose*, episode 385, Voice America, On Becoming an Inspiring, Loving, Servant Leader, June 22, 2022.

[4] Steinkruger, *Inspiration Universal and Unlimited* (2022), pp. 122–123.

[5] Hare, *Lead Brighter* (2020).

[6] Chapman & Sisodia, *Everybody Matters* (2015), p. 116.

[7] Garcia & Miralles, *The Book of Ichigo Ichie* (2019), p. 3.

[8] Gutknecht & Lahey, *Meaning at Work* (2017).

[9] The idea of leadership being about communicating worth and potential is informed through this book and its authors: Covey & Covey Haller, *Live Life in Crescendo* (2022).

[10] Gutknecht & Lahey, *Meaning at Work* (2017), p. 72.

[11] Cortez, *Purpose Ignited* (2020).

[12] Barnes, *Ikigai* (2018).

[13] Steinkruger, *Inspiration Universal and Unlimited* (2022).

[14] *Working on Purpose*, episode 325, Voice America, April 28, 2021.

[15] The concept "love-in-work" is from Buckingham & Goodall, *Nine Lies About Work* (2019).

[16] Goins, *The Art of Work* (2015), p. 145.

[17] *Working on Purpose*, episode 228, Voice America, June 19, 2019.

[18] Bhatnagar & Minukas, *Unfear* (2022), p. 4.

[19] Bhatnagar & Minukas, *Unfear* (2022).

[20] Bhatnagar & Minukas, *Unfear* (2022), p. 43.

[21] Bhatnagar & Minukas, *Unfear* (2022), p. xix.

[22] Cutting, *Employees First!* (2022).

[23] To dig more deeply into the dynamics and presence of fear, I suggest looking into Bhatnagar and Minukas' eight archetypes of fear, which they discuss in Bhatnagar & Minukas, *Unfear* (2022), p. 72.

[24] Baird & Sullivan, *Leading with Heart* (2022).

[25] Bhatnagar & Minukas, *Unfear* (2022), p. 3.

[26] Baird & Sullivan, *Leading with Heart* (2022), see p. 72 for more details of the origination of the unfear concept.

[27] Baird & Sullivan, *Leading with Heart* (2022), p. 94.

[28] Baird & Sullivan, *Leading with Heart* (2022).

[29] Baird & Sullivan, *Leading with Heart* (2022).

[30] Esfahani Smith, *The Power of Meaning* (2017), p. 96.

[31] Boccalandro, *Do Good at Work* (2021), p. 41.

[32] Boccalandro, *Do Good at Work* (2021).

[33] Clifton & Harter, *Wellbeing at Work* (2021).

[34] Boccalandro, *Do Good at Work* (2021), p. 8.

[35] Mercurio, *The Invisible Leader* (2017).

[36] McDonald, *It's Time to Talk about Race at Work* (2021).

[37] Covey & Covey Haller, *Live Life in Crescendo* (2022), p. 95.

[38] McDonald, *It's Time to Talk about Race at Work* (2021), p. 56.

[39] McDonald, *It's Time to Talk about Race at Work* (2021), p. 50.

[40] McDonald, *It's Time to Talk about Race at Work* (2021), Inc, p. 27.

Chapter 8

[1] Kegan & Lahey, *An Everyone Culture* (2016).

[2] Wolfe, *The Living Organization* (2011); Wolfe's consulting company Quantum uses the SQi assessment from Deep Change to measure spiritual intelligence.

[3] Morris, *The Beautiful Business* (2021), p. 234.

[4] Morris, *The Beautiful Business* (2021), p. 23.

[5] Morris, *The Beautiful Business* (2021), p. 40.

[6] Morris, *The Beautiful Business* (2021), p. 133.

[7] Spiker, *The Only Leaders Worth Following* (2020), p. 25.

[8] Firth & Zintz, *Grit, Grace & Gravitas* (2020).

[9] *Working on Purpose*, episode 308, Voice America, December 30, 2020.

[10] Spiker, *The Only Leaders Worth Following* (2020), pp. 71–72.

[11] Spiker, *The Only Leaders Worth Following* (2020), pp. 32–33.

[12] Spiker, *The Only Leaders Worth Following* (2020), p. 135.

[13] Morris, *The Beautiful Business* (2021), p. 298.

[14] Sisodia & Gelb, *The HEALING Organization* (2019).

[15] Woods, *The Golden Thread* (2020).

[16] Woods, *The Golden Thread* (2020), p. 299.

[17] *Working on Purpose*, episode 194, Voice America, Reviving Passion in Corporate America, October 24, 2018.

[18] Ciaramicoli & Crystal, *The Soulful Leader* (2019), Introduction section.

[19] Listen to the conversation with Dr. Arthur Ciaramicoli about his book on soulful leadership here: *Working on Purpose*, episode 215, Voice America, Soulful Leadership Creates Connection and Competitive Advantage, March 20, 2019.

[20] Morris, *The Beautiful Business* (2021), see discussion on p. 94.

[21] *Working on Purpose*, episode 385, iHeart Radio, On Becoming an Inspiring, Loving, Servant Leader, June 16, 2022.

[22] Steinkruger, *Inspiration Universal and Unlimited* (2022).

[23] Steinkruger, *Inspiration Universal and Unlimited* (2022), pp. 48–49.

[24] Buckingham & Goodall, *Nine Lies About Work* (2019), p. 20.

[25] *How the Grinch Stole Christmas*, directed by Ron Howard and starring Jim Carrey and Taylor Momsen, released November 17, 2000.

[26] Gutknecht & Lahey, *Meaning at Work* (2017).

[27] Gulati, *Deep Purpose* (2022), pp. 75–76.

[28] Gulati, *Deep Purpose* (2022), p. 73.

[29] Morris, *The Beautiful Business* (2021), p. 215.

[30] Gulati, *Deep Purpose* (2022).

[31] Coleman, *HBR Guide to Crafting Your Purpose* (2022).

[32] *Working on Purpose*, episode 365, Voice America, February 2, 2022.

[33] Morris, *The Beautiful Business* (2021), p. 215.

[34] Gulati, *Deep Purpose* (2022).

[35] Cortez, *Purpose Ignited* (2020).

[36] Gulati, *Deep Purpose* (2022), p. 98.

[37] Gulati, *Deep Purpose* (2022), pp. 98–99.

[38] www.toastmasters.org

[39] Perform a search for your local improv clubs to see what classes they offer. As an example, this is the Dallas-based comedy club I've taken classes with: https://dallas-comedyclub.com

[40] Smith & Lewis, *Both/And Thinking* (2022).

[41] Goins, *The Art of Work* (2015), p. 169.

[42] Efron, *Purpose Meets Execution* (2017), p. 83.

[43] *Working on Purpose*, episode 210, Voice America, February 13, 2019. Check out his book: Craig, *Leading from Purpose* (2018).

[44] Chapman & Sisodia, *Everybody Matters* (2015), pp. 240–241.

[45] Hare, *Lead Brighter* (2020), p. 55.

[46] Morris, *The Beautiful Business* (2021).

[47] The "L" word is making an appearance more frequently in business today. This book, written by a man who spent 50 years in a healthcare career, 25 of which as a CEO, puts love as a central tenet in leadership today: Steinkruger, *Inspiration Universal and Unlimited* (2022).

[48] Morris, *The Beautiful Business* (2021), p. 43, emphasis added.

[49] Morris, *The Beautiful Business* (2021), p. 226.

[50] Morris, *The Beautiful Business* (2021), pp. 26–28.

[51] Morris, *The Beautiful Business* (2021), p. 257.

[52] Morris, *The Beautiful Business* (2021), p. 125, paraphrased.

[53] *Working on Purpose*, A. Cortez, B Corps: Business as a Force for Profit and Purpose, July 14, 2021.

[54] Morris, *The Beautiful Business* (2021).

[55] Elgin, "Humanity's Journey Home" (2017), p. 146.

[56] Plotkin, "The Realm of Purpose Least Realized" (2017).
[57] Peele, *Planet on Purpose* (2018), p. 184.
[58] Peele, *Planet on Purpose* (2018), p. 188.
[59] Peele, *Planet on Purpose* (2018), p. 189.
[60] Frankl, *Man's Search for Meaning* (2006).
[61] Peele, *Planet on Purpose* (2018), p. 157.
[62] Kuntzelman & DiPerna, *Purpose Rising* (2017), p. 3.
[63] Skinner, *The Purpose Upgrade* (2022).

Conclusion

[1] Morris, *The Beautiful Business* (2021).

Index

A
Airbnb 95
Anderson, Ray 41
Angelou, Maya 92
Antis, Charles 74
apathy 49
appreciation 92, 150
artificial intelligence (AI),
    leveraging 98–100
attitudinal way of finding meaning
    52
Austin, J. Paul 43–44
autonomy 86

B
B Corp companies 154
Baird, John 118–119
beautiful business 11–13, 73,
    150–154
Beeny, Claudia 112–113
belonging 122–124
Bhatnagar, G. 117
Boccalandro, Bea 120
boredom 49, 98
"both/and" mindset 10, 132, 147
Brown, Brene 154
Buckingham, Marcus 89
burnout 27, 28
Business Roundtable 2, 9–10, 13

C
Calderoni, Frank 42, 43, 44,
    124–125
caring leaders 107–108
Chapman, Bob 90, 107
Ciaramicoli, Arthur 137

Clifton, J. 28
Cohen, Rabbi Daniel 62
Coleman, John 144
collective effervescence 154
color-blind workplace *see* DEIB
    (diversity, equity, inclusion,
    and belonging)
command and control procedure 85
community
  and organization's purpose 74
  significance of 154
company character 42–43, 125
company's purpose 140–146
  elevating with beauty 150–154
  embedding in operational aspect
    146–148
  see also purpose
compensation policies 86–87
conscious capitalism 2, 8–11
consciousness, and purpose 66
cosmosapien 155–157, 165
Covey, Stephen R. 122
COVID pandemic, impact of 25,
    40, 78–79, 165
Craig, Nick 150
creative way of finding meaning 52
customers
  and organization's purpose
    72–73
  significance of 153

D
deep purpose 133, 146, 147, 157
DEIB (diversity, equity, inclusion,
    and belonging) 122–124
depression 48

doing the work 133–136
Domani, Ayala 81
dress codes 87
Dundon, Elaine 50, 58

E
eco-awakening 36, 158
Economics of Mattering 121
Efron, Louis 72, 149
Elgin, Duane 39–41
emotions and emotional
        intelligence (EQ) 80 105
    and caring leaders 107–108
    and DEIB 122–124
    ESG+R Standard 124–126
    fear and toxicity 116–119
    and feelings, difference between
        105–106
    joy 115–116
    love in work 115–116
    managing through meaning
        108–112
    and passion 112–113
    social and job purposing 119–121
empathic listening 107
employees, and organization's
        purpose 71–72
environmental sustainability 41
environmental, social, and
        governance (ESG), as
        business imperative 41–44
    see also ESG+R Standard
Esfahani Smith, Emily 48
ESG+R Standard 124–126
"everybody matters" caring
        approach 107–108
evolution 133, 136, 138
experiential way of finding
        meaning 52

F
fear 105–106, 116–119
feedback 91–93

feelings 105–106
Firth, Jane 133
forced ranking 87
Frankl, Viktor 49, 50, 54–55, 131

G
Gelb, Michael 135, 145
Goodall, Ashley 89
Grayson, David 37–38
Gulati, Ranjay 13, 27, 42, 57–58,
        64, 94–95, 140, 157
gumption 5–6, 163
    beautiful business, intelligent
        design 11–13
    business as living organization
        6–8
    and conscious capitalism 8–11
    long play in business 13–16

H
Haar, Ellie ter 36
Haller, Cynthia Covey 122
happiness, and meaning 52–53
Hare, Alicia 8, 62–63
Harter, J. 28
holacracy 86
House of Shine 113
Hoyos, K. 67
human capital audit 85–87
Hurst, Aaron 66
hybrid work 29, 30–31, 97

I
ichigo ichie 109
IKEA 41
ikigai 112
individual strengths 87–89
inspirational leaders 108, 137–139
integrated system 40
intelligence quotient (IQ) 79–80, 84
investors
    and organization's purpose 74
    significance of 154

J
job purposing 119–121
Jones, Tim 67–68
joy 115–116

K
Kennedy, J. F. 24
Klotz, Anthony 23, 26
Knudstorp, Jørgen Vig 140

L
Learning Organization (Senge) 57
Levy, Michael 92
living economy 38–41
living organization, business as
        6–8, 37–38, 61
local workplace 96
logotherapy 47, 49–53, 54, 58, 110
long play in business 13–16
long-term growth 14–15
Long-Term Stock Exchange
        (LTSE) 15
love in work 113–116
Lynn, Sheryl 115

M
Mainwaring, Simon 38
managing through meaning
        108–112
Managing Through Meaning™
        109, 110
mastery, importance of 114
Mattiske, Catherine 29–30, 97
maturation 133
McClay, Diane 70
meaning 47–48, 52, 146, 163
    crisis of 48
    deep meaning 48–49
    managing through 108–112
    motivating through 56–59
    in organizations 54–56
    see also logotherapy

meaning maintenance model 57–58
MEANINGology 50
mental health 27–29
Mercurio, Zach 62, 121
Milano, Gregory 14, 69, 86–87
mindset 108
Minukas, M. 117
Mitchell, Melerick 115
momentum 89–91
Morris, Steven 11, 13, 132, 138,
        151–152
motivation, through meaning
        56–59
My Octopus Teacher (documentary)
        36

N
nurture 164
    employee engagement and
        fulfillment 93–94
    feedback and recognition 91–93
    high performance versus
        momentum 89–91
    human capital audit 85–87
    individual strengths 87–89
    leveraging AI and robotics
        98–100
    and time and place
        deconstruction 94–98

O
obsoledge 22, 85
on-site work 31
opening the hearts 164–165
ownership 61–62, 164
    see also purpose

P
pandemic epiphanies 26
parking lot attendant, job
        purposing 120
passion 108, 112–113, 115, 137

Pattakos, Alex 50, 58
Peele, Brandon 25–26, 63, 67, 156
performance outcomes 29
personal aspects for leaders 11–12
place of work, deconstruction of
    94–98
planet, and organization's purpose
    74–75
potentiality, employee segregation
    based on 89
proof of purpose (POP) 165
purpose 61–62, 163
    benefits 71
    and community/society 74
    of company *see* company's
        purpose
    and consciousness 66
    and customers 72–73
    deep 70–71
    and employees 71–72
    and investors 74
    meaning and significance of
        62–65
    parliament of 68–75
    and planet 74–75
    and suppliers 73–74
    of team members 148–150
    in today's business 66–68
purpose economy 62, 66
purpose washing 64
purposeful behavior 10

R
racial justice 44
    see also DEIB (diversity, equity,
        inclusion, and belonging)
recognition 91–93, 107
reflection 107
relational connection 122–124
remote work 29, 30–31, 95
residual cash earnings 87
responsibility 59

responsibleness 111
Ries, Eric 15
robotics, leveraging 98–100

S
Sangwan, Neha 9, 20
Scheler, Max 36
Secretan, Lance 137
seeing choice 110–111
self-inquiry 134
self-transcendence 111
Seligman, Martin 25
Senge, Peter 57
sharing 107
Shore, Howard 68, 72
short-termism 13–15
silence 24
Sisodia, Raj 8–9, 10, 135, 145
Skinner, Paul 158
social injustice 43
social purposing 119–121
society, and organization's purpose
    74
soul 131–132, 165
    and company's purpose *see*
        company's purpose
    doing the work 133–136
    and inspirational leaders 137–
        139
    and syntropy mindset 155–158
    and team members' purpose
        148–150
Spiker, Tim 134–135
spikiness 88–89
spiritual intelligence (SQ) 80–81
stakeholder capitalism 9–10, 13,
    37–38
static work schedules 87
Steinkruger, Roger 91, 107, 138–
    139
storytelling 118–119, 146–147
Stryker 72

suicide rates 48
Sullivan, Edward 118–119
superordinate goals 68–69
suppliers
    and organization's purpose
        73–74
    significance of 154
sustainability 33–35, 163–164
    as business imperative 41–44
    ego economy and living economy
        38–41
    and living organization 37–38
    and wisdom 35–37
syntropy mindset 155–158
system thinking 34

T
talent, nurturing 89–90
team members
    purpose of 148–150
    significance of 153
technology 98–100
telecommuting restrictions 87
therapy 47–48, 164
    and deep meaning 48–49
    motivating through meaning
        56–59
    logotherapy *see* logotherapy
    and organizations 54–56
Thiyagarajan, Swati 36
time, deconstruction of 94–98
toxicity 116–119
training and coaching programs 136
transcendent business experiences
    151–152

transformational model 142–144
truth 110

U
uniqueness 111
upstanding company character
    42–43
urgency 19–20, 163
    well-being 27–29
    workforce requirements 21–23
    work-life harmony 23–27
    work location and timing 29–31

V
virtual workplace 97
Vitally Inspired leadership program
    136

W
wake the soul (SQ) 131–133, 165
    see also soul
well-being 27–29
Wells Fargo 86
Westphal, Deborah 7, 9, 21, 85
Whole Foods 73
wisdom 35–37
Wolfe, Norman 7, 37
Woods, Holly 63, 72, 136
workforce requirements 21–23
work-life harmony 23–27
work location and timing 29–31
work task flow 86

Z
Zintz, Andrea 133

CPSIA information can be obtained
at www.ICGtesting.com
Printed in the USA
JSHW031324030223
37197JS00002B/8